Lunar Living

Lunar Living

Working with
the magic of
the moon cycles

KIRSTY GALLAGHER

yellow
kite

First published in Great Britain in 2020 by Yellow Kite
An imprint of Hodder & Stoughton
An Hachette UK company

8

Copyright © Kirsty Gallagher 2020

The right of Kirsty Gallagher to be identified as the Author
of the Work has been asserted by her in accordance with the
Copyright, Designs and Patents Act 1988.

Illustrations by The Colour Study © Hodder & Stoughton 2020

A CIP catalogue record for this title is available from the British Library

Hardback ISBN 978 1 529 39820 5
eBook ISBN 978 1 529 39822 9

Typeset in Celeste 11/15.5 pt by
Palimpsest Book Production Limited, Falkirk, Stirlingshire

Printed and bound in Great Britain by Clays Ltd, Elcograf S.p.A.

Hodder & Stoughton policy is to use papers that are natural,
renewable and recyclable products and made from wood grown in
sustainable forests. The logging and manufacturing processes are expected
to conform to the environmental regulations of the country of origin.

Yellow Kite
Hodder & Stoughton Ltd
Carmelite House
50 Victoria Embankment
London EC4Y 0DZ

www.yellowkitebooks.co.uk

This book is dedicated to my incredible mum, Sandy G, and my darling best friend, Samantha Day, both of whom have always believed in how bright I can shine.

Contents

• • •

Introduction

• • •

WELCOME TO LUNAR LIVING!

Have you ever woken up feeling overly emotional and nothing can shake you out of it all day? Have you ever found yourself, out of nowhere, obsessing over certain areas of your life for no apparent reason? Are there days when your intuition or gut feeling are so loud and so strong that all the answers and changes that need to be made in your life seem to have become obvious and the way ahead is clear? Are there times when you can't sleep and end up lying awake all night? What about those days when synchronicities seem constant and everything falls into place like magic? And days when you feel the need to be completely alone, craving quiet time and solitude?

What if I told you that all these things and much more can be explained by working with the constantly changing cycles of the moon? That rather than being thrown around by your thoughts and emotions, you could instead look to the moon and her ancient wisdom to make sense of how you are feeling, and use her cycles to create powerful change and take back control of your life? This is the magic of the moon and it's what *Lunar Living* will provide.

For those of you who don't know me, my name is Kirsty Gallagher and I will be your moon mentor, revealing my moon musings to bring clear guidance on how you can work with the mystical, magical energies of the moon.

Looking back, I've always been fascinated by the moon and astrology. I remember as a teenager poring over astrology books to find out about my sun and moon signs and how they relate to me as a person.

In 2009, I spent eight months in India, immersed in my yoga teacher training and on a real soul journey, during which time the moon came to be one of my greatest teachers. It is traditional not to practise yoga on the full and new moons and during these 'days off', I experienced the profound effects of the moon. I actually felt things shift on moon days: the energy differed, people's moods and personalities noticeably changed – and my love affair with the moon began.

Moon days were for self-care, self-reflection and deep inner work. These days of quiet contemplation allowed me to fully connect to and draw upon the energies of the moon and immerse myself in her wisdom, effects and guidance – a turning point, a time of insights and answers, clarification and intention-setting, with deep stirrings in my heart and soul. These twice-monthly check-ins showed me areas in my life that needed work or attention, what was coming to the surface for me and, most of all, the power I had over the direction of my own life.

Over those eight months (and ever since), I made profound shifts in my life working with the moon – recalibrating, resetting and realigning my inner compass – and I now want to share the wisdom I gained with you.

You may already have heard about the magic of the moon. Maybe you've been captivated by the sight of her in the night sky. Perhaps you've noticed your moods – or those of the people around you – changing at certain times of the month. Or maybe you want a way to honour the passing of time, an opportunity for a regular check-in, to get in tune with a cycle, a rhythm, a flow in your life or to take back control.

Whatever your reasons, there is something for you in this book and its potent power lies in its simplicity: you don't have to know your sun, moon or ascending sign or which of your houses the moon happens to fall in (although this is all fascinating); you don't need to follow a certain spiritual path or even believe in astrology – or anything in particular; and everyone can gain huge insights and inspiration, making quantum leaps in their lives, all from working with the phases of the moon.

My motivation for writing this book was largely the many responses to the shares of my moon musings on social media and daily requests for more information on working with lunar energies. This encouraged me to create Lunar Living, an online sisterhood where we learn to follow the moon's guidance and wisdom, and we celebrate all the moon magic. So many people have been awakened to the power and the incredible influence of the moon and the skies; around the days of the full moon, social media is littered with talk about sleepless nights, the moon now features in everything from jewellery to clothing and Mercury retrograde is a commonly talked about and accepted phenomenon.

But the real turning point came when I did an on-stage talk at the Birmingham Mind Body Spirit Festival in October 2016. I expected a handful of people to show up, but ended up with a crowd of hundreds of people – from businessmen to mums to teenage girls and older men – all eager to hear what I had to say. At the end of that presentation (and at every talk or workshop I have held since), there was a long queue of people wanting to ask questions or tell their stories. This made me realise that people of all ages, from all backgrounds and in all walks of life are actively seeking a reconnection to cycles, to nature, to understanding rhythms, to receiving guidance and, ultimately, a different way to live.

Hundreds of people that day (and countless since) asked if I could recommend a book to help them learn more and delve deeper. So here it is! *Lunar Living* provides an understanding of emotional impulses, allows a time to be and a time to do and gives you back control of your life – an opportunity, month on month, to hold yourself accountable and work with an ancient magic and cycle. And within these pages are the answers that all those people – and you, as you are holding this book – are seeking.

I will show you how to work with each phase of the moon, using them to your advantage, along with the influences of the zodiac signs, the wisdom the moon wants to share with you and how to work with her cycles and energies to know yourself better than ever before, bringing about real transformation in your life. Even just skimming the surface will bring you a deeper understanding of your own and other people's behaviours at different times of the month and will help you to go with the flow of life, instead of constantly pushing against it.

Making ancient mystical practices and wisdom relevant to modern-day life is my passion; I want *Lunar Living* to be accessible and for moon magic to fit effortlessly into your daily life, so that you can experience the profound effects and reap the benefits. That's why at the end of each chapter in Parts I and III you'll find a 'Moon magic made easy' feature – a quick, at-a-glance summary, especially for those times when you want just enough to make a difference without having to dig too deep.

You will also find that I refer to the moon as 'she' or 'her'. This is because the moon is the feminine energy of the universe that connects us to our inner world, our intuition, dreams and the call of our souls. After working with her for ten years, I feel that I know her well enough to be that familiar with her. And my deepest wish is that you'll get to know her well enough too.

Delve into *Lunar Living* with an open heart and mind and allow the moon to be a guide for you.

I am so excited to be sharing this lunar journey with you. With lunar love and moon magic,
Kirsty

PART I:

Moon Magic

CHAPTER 1:

Understanding the Simple Science

THIS IS NOT an astrology or science book. It is a book about the moon, her magic and how to weave it into your life. But I want you to have enough information to be able to understand the basics of astrology and the moon without diluting the magic. So here goes . . .

As the earth moves around the sun, the moon moves around the earth. The moon is the earth's only natural satellite. She is a very wise old soul with an estimated age of 4.51 billion years.

In keeping with her magical, mystical energy we still aren't completely sure where the moon came from. The most popular theory is that she was formed when a huge Mars-sized planet named Theia collided with the earth at 10,000mph. The debris from the two planets orbited the earth before coalescing into the moon. Newer findings have suggested that the moon's composition is almost entirely identical to the earth's, throwing this theory into question. And so the mysteries of the moon continue.

THE LIGHT OF THE MOON

The moon does not produce any light, which can be hard to believe if you have ever gazed up at the bright full moon in the sky – but what you are seeing is the reflection of the sun on the moon's surface.

During a new moon (where there is no moon in the sky) the sun, moon and earth are positioned in a straight line, with the moon passing between the other two. As this happens, the sun is shining light on the side of the moon we cannot see, making it seem as if she is no longer in the sky. During a full moon the moon and sun are on opposite sides of the earth, meaning that the light of the sun fully illuminates the side of the moon's surface that we can see, making her appear bright and beautiful in the sky.

It is also the reflection of the sun on the moon's surface that makes her appear to change shape in the sky on a nightly basis, when in fact she is always whole. The position of the moon in relation to the earth and the sun means that we see a different portion of her lit as she moves around the earth each month. This is what is known as the moon's phases.

THE LUNAR CYCLE

You may have heard that a moon cycle takes between 27 and 29.5 days. Here's why . . .

It takes 27 days, 7 hours and 43 minutes (27.3 days for ease) for the moon to complete one full orbit around the earth relative to fixed stars. This is known as the sidereal orbit or sidereal month.

However, when we talk about a lunar month we are referring to the time it takes the moon to go from new back to new again; this averages 29 days, 12 hours and 44 minutes, but can vary by up to 6 hours each way, so let's say 29.5 days. This is called a synodic month and the reason why it is slightly longer than the sidereal month is because it is determined by the position of the moon in relation to the sun. Remember that a new moon occurs when the sun, moon and earth are positioned in a straight line, with the moon between the earth and the sun. As the moon moves around earth, the earth is also moving around the sun, and so the moon has to travel 360° and then a further 30° each month to catch up and realign with the earth and the sun to become new once more.

This makes a 'lunar year' only 354 days, which is out of alignment with our 365-day calendar year by 11 days a year. This is why most years there will be 25 moons in a calendar year – 12 new and 13 full or vice versa.

THE GRAVITATIONAL PULL OF THE MOON

Many of us are aware that the gravitational pull of the moon causes the daily tides of the oceans and seas; this is called tidal force. The moon's gravity pulls the earth and its water towards her, causing our high and low tides. It's also this gravitational pull that stabilises the earth's axis, creating seasons. Research has shown that the gravitational pull of the moon slows down the earth's rotation, giving our days their 24-hour format. Without it, a day would only be approximately eight hours long.

THE ZODIAC SIGNS AND SEASONS

Based on Western astrology, the sun stays in each of the 12 zodiac signs for around a month. The date on which the sun enters/leaves the sign is roughly the same every year; however, it can change by a day or so either side, year on year. The astrological new year begins with Aries season, around 21 March, which marks the spring equinox. The period of time the sun spends in a sign is commonly known as a season, so between 21 March and 19 April we would be in Aries season, then 20 April to 20 May is Taurus season and so on through the year as we move through each sign of the zodiac.

At some point during each season, there will be a new and a full moon; they can fall at any time within that season. Imagine the sky as a big circle divided into 12 pieces, each representing a zodiac sign, with the earth in the centre. The new moon will fall in the same sign as the zodiac season we are currently in, as the sun and moon are in the same place (zodiac sign) in the sky. On a full moon, the moon is on the opposite side of the earth to the sun, so will fall in the zodiac sign opposite the sun in the sky. The table opposite should make this a bit clearer.

Everyone on earth sees the moon phases on the same day, however the Southern and Northern Hemispheres see the moon positioned in opposite ways. To our Southern Hemisphere readers, please note that the seasons on the table opposite will be the opposite way round.

Aries 21 March–19 April Spring Equinox as sun moves into Aries **Element:** Fire **Quality:** Cardinal – begins spring New Moon Aries (Cardinal – begins) Full Moon Libra (Cardinal – begins)	**Libra 23 Sep–22 Oct** Autumn Equinox as sun moves into Libra **Element:** Air **Quality:** Cardinal – begins autumn New Moon Libra (Cardinal – begins) Full Moon Aries (Cardinal – begins)

Taurus 20 Apr–20 May **Element:** Earth **Quality:** Fixed – stabilises spring New Moon Taurus (Fixed – middle) Full Moon Scorpio (Fixed – middle)	**Scorpio 23 Oct–21 Nov** **Element:** Water **Quality:** Fixed – stabilises autumn New Moon Scorpio (Fixed – middle) Full Moon Taurus (Fixed – middle)

Gemini 21 May–20 Jun **Element:** Air **Quality:** Mutable – ends spring New Moon Gemini (Mutable – ends) Full Moon Sagittarius (Mutable – ends)	**Sagittarius 22 Nov–21 Dec** **Element:** Fire **Quality:** Mutable – ends autumn New Moon Sagittarius (Mutable – ends) Full Moon Gemini (Mutable – ends)

Cancer 21 Jun–22 Jul Summer Solstice as sun moves into Cancer **Element:** Water **Quality:** Cardinal – begins summer New Moon Cancer (Cardinal – begins) Full Moon Capricorn (Cardinal – begins)	**Capricorn 22 Dec–19 Jan** Winter Solstice as sun moves into Capricorn **Element:** Earth **Quality:** Cardinal – begins winter New Moon Capricorn (Cardinal – begins) Full Moon Cancer (Cardinal – begins)

Leo 23 Jul–22 Aug **Element:** Fire **Quality:** Fixed – stabilises summer New Moon Leo (Fixed – middle) Full Moon Aquarius (Fixed – middle)	**Aquarius 20 Jan–18 Feb** **Element:** Air **Quality:** Fixed – stabilises winter New Moon Aquarius (Fixed – middle) Full Moon Leo (Fixed – middle)

Virgo 23 Aug–22 Sep **Element:** Earth **Quality:** Mutable – ends summer New Moon Virgo (Mutable – ends) Full Moon Pisces (Mutable – ends)	**Pisces 19 Feb–20 Mar** **Element:** Water **Quality:** Mutable – ends winter New Moon Pisces (Mutable – ends) Full Moon Virgo (Mutable – ends)

SCIENCE VS MAGIC

Our ancestors believed in the power of the moon; the *Farmers' Almanac* and astrologers believe too. Yet plenty of scientists and researchers over the years have set out to disprove it. The only proof I can offer you comes from ten years of first-hand experience of working with the moon, and the profound effect this has had on my life. And not just my life, but those of the many people my Moon Musings and Lunar Living teachings have resonated with over the years, who have shared their stories with me.

What we are working with here is magic, not science. And the only proof you need lies in the practice of Lunar Living – in trying it for yourself and experiencing first-hand the magical benefits that this way of living brings to your life.

Now we've looked a little at the science, let's delve into the ancient magic of the moon . . .

Moon magic made easy

✴ As the earth moves around the sun, the moon moves around the earth.

✴ A new moon happens when the moon passes between earth and the sun, and the sun shines light on the side of the moon we cannot see, so she seems to 'disappear' from the sky.

✴ A full moon occurs when the moon and sun are on opposite sides of the earth, meaning that the light of the sun fully illuminates the side of the moon's surface that we can see.

✴ A lunar cycle is approximately 29.5 days – the time it takes from one new moon to the next.

✴ The sun moves through a different zodiac sign approximately every 30 days; during that zodiac season the new moon will fall in the same zodiac sign and the full moon in the opposite sign.

CHAPTER 2:
The Magic of the Moon and Lunar Living

'And above all, watch with glittering eyes the whole world around you because the greatest secrets are always hidden in the most unlikely places. Those who don't believe in magic will never find it.'

Extract from *The Minpins* by Roald Dahl (1991)

WE ARE ALL aware of the moon. For many nights of each month she is there, visible in the sky above us shining down her ethereal, otherworldly light. We've all, no doubt, at some point been captivated by the arresting sight of a full moon, rooting us to the spot, as something stirs within. We may have even heard people speak of the effects of a full moon and how it affects emotions, sleep patterns and state of mind.

In ancient times, the moon was the marker of the passage of time and our ancestors looked to her for insights and wisdom, using her phases for gathering, sharing and ritual. This shows how, at one time, we were much more tuned in to the moon, and her gravitational pull that moves not only the tides, but also our energy levels and the watery inner world of our emotions and dreams.

In our fast-paced modern-day life we seem to have become distanced from this concept. As life has become more 'man-made' we have lost touch with the power of nature, with a natural rhythm, an ebb and a flow, a wax and a wane, and at the same time, our intuition, our insight and our inner powers. We have swapped ritual for routine. We have forgotten that there is a time to grow and a time to rest, a time of high-energy activity and a time to be still, gather and pause.

We have tried to make life linear, but that's not the way it is. We have forgotten that we too are part of nature and that nature is cyclic and in a constant state of flow; and as we resist and fight against this flow, life loses much of its meaning.

But we can take back control. Lunar Living brings us home to ourselves, our dreams and visions and goals, month after month. Working with the magic of the moon is a tool of immense self-awareness, self-care, nourishment, empower- ment, manifestation and purpose. Below are some of the many ways that Lunar Living and the moon will weave their magic into your life.

SELF-CARE FOR THE SOUL

One of the moon's biggest teachings is that there is a time to be and a time to do. Even the moon doesn't shine at her brightest 365 days of the year, showing us that if we don't take time out to rest, we'll have no energy, inspiration or motivation when it's our time to shine!

We are in a 'busy' epidemic right now. Always on, always contactable, dangerously glamourising the fact that we have full schedules and so much to do.

Remember the Isaac Newton theory that what goes up must come down? The same applies to our energy and stress levels. If we don't balance out being busy and doing with rest and being, eventually we will crash and burn. Burnout, anxiety, unhappiness and stress are at an all-time high, but it doesn't need to be this way.

Do you, like most people, have a packed social and work calendar, a family with lots of demands, a mind that never switches off or you are always taking care of and giving your time and energy away to everyone else around you? Tiredness, exhaustion, overwhelm, begrudgingly saying yes, feeling taken advantage of, snapping and losing it when it all gets too much are all sure signs that something is out of alignment and you are in need of some self-care and time out.

Coming back into a cycle, a rhythm and taking care of you and your needs, even if that's just twice a month, will make the biggest difference to how you feel, act and react the rest of the time. Lunar Living will be life-changing for you – it offers you not only time, but also the space to get to the bottom of why you are feeling and living this way. Very often, always being busy is a way to distract from what is really going on in your life. Always saying yes has undertones of people-pleasing and being afraid to say no. Tiredness and overwhelm come from never being able to switch off and truly relax, instead thinking you should always be doing something and feeling guilty if you're not.

By disappearing from the sky for a few nights every month, the moon shows with beautiful simplicity – and without guilt – that in order to shine and be your best, to be full and powerful, you simply have to take that time out: say no, practise self-care and, at times, withdraw into yourself to fulfil your own needs.

Of course, you may not be able to ask your boss for a day off for rest and self-care on the dark moon, but living in alignment with the moons phases gives you permission to do this. You can ensure that in your diary you've blocked out some alone time, even if that's just an hour to lock yourself away in the bathroom and take a long, hot bath. Simple changes like this will make the biggest difference to your life.

Lunar Living can be such a powerful tool in forward planning too. You will no longer be taken by surprise by waves of raw emotion, finding yourself in the depths of despair and reacting from those depths. Instead, being aware that the new or full moon is coming, you can carve out time for yourself – for self-awareness and self-care – around these moon times.

To simply be with what you are experiencing and what it is showing you – this alone is a powerful way to own your experience and makes you less likely to blame everyone or everything else (except maybe the moon!). And as you take responsibility for how you are feeling, you take back control of your life.

You owe it to yourself and all those around you to exercise self-care and nurture your soul. And if you are too busy to take a day, or even just a few hours, out once or twice a month to rest, reflect, reconnect and recalibrate, then you – more than anyone – need Lunar Living!

TRUST IN THE MOON – AND YOU

Lunar Living gives us trust in something greater – a guiding force and ancient wisdom that were here long before we were and will be here long after we've gone.

As we begin to live back in alignment with this ancient power, one of the greatest gifts of Lunar Living is the ability to believe and trust in yourself. This is an invaluable self-help and self-awareness tool for our modern-day world.

How many of us know what we actually want? You could no doubt tell me in great detail what you don't want. But do you know what you really *do* want in life? Adulting often sees us forgetting our dreams for the sake of doing what 'should' be done, allowing our lives to be dictated by so many external influences and factors and ifs, buts and maybes.

If you are honest with yourself, the likelihood is that you have been getting inner niggles for a long time. The little voice that tells you that you're not in the right job, your relationship isn't working or your focus is in the wrong place. That inner 'knowing' that there is 'something more'. A recurring feeling of sadness, low-level anxiety, loneliness, frustration or the array of other emotions that signpost you to discontent in your life.

But the less you listen to the inner niggles and intuitive

nudges, the smaller you get, and the quieter the voice of your intuition, your heart and your soul become. Every time you ignore a nudge from the Universe or make an excuse or give in to a fear, you shrink a little more, subconsciously telling yourself that you don't trust yourself, or your dreams – or life.

That's where the moon holds such power: rather than just ignoring these emotions you start to work with the moon's cycles and phases, understanding, tuning into and acting on the flow of the emotional tides that the moon helps you to uncover. As you do this every month, it helps you to reawaken your intuition and the whisper of your soul, giving you the opportunity to tune in to what you want – what you really want. This, in turn, helps you to set things in motion and look for the signs, seeing them everywhere, following where they lead you. You become brave enough to let go of things that aren't serving you – your doubts and your fears – and you start to trust in the bigger picture, even if you can't see it yet. Then magic starts to happen, things change and you develop a trust so deep in yourself that you no longer need to look outside for answers, guidance or validation; instead you find this deep, intuitive inner knowing within you.

TUNING INTO YOUR EMOTIONAL MOONSCAPE

As we've learned, the moon turns the tides, keeps the earth on its axis and gives us seasons, and her gravitational pull is what gives a day its 24-hour structure. It stands to reason, given all of this, and the fact that we are made up of approximately 60 per cent water, that the moon would exert the same gravitational pull on the watery inner world of our emotions, intuition, dreams and the call of the soul. Just like the tides, the moon draws us down and pulls to the forefront all that hides beneath our awareness so that we can become conscious of it.

One thing us humans are skilled at is telling everyone that we are fine, when beneath the surface we are in turmoil. We numb emotions, we suppress, deny, run and hide from them. For some of us, it may be that we are simply 'too busy' to stop and check in with how we actually feel and so we lose touch with our inner worlds. Or, somewhere along the way, we have come to label our feelings and believe it's not acceptable to feel angry or show too much emotion, and it's 'good' to feel happy and joyful.

But we can't selectively feel emotions. If we try to deny anger and pain, we will also numb out happiness and joy, and that's where we become blocked and inauthentic. Every time we hold back tears, hide our pain or don't express our hurt, we deny ourselves healing and authenticity. Our emotions are the key to inner growth and transformation. But first we need to get in touch with *what* we are feeling: we have to feel it to heal it.

The moon pulls our emotions to the surface to show us clearly where we need to make changes in our lives. We often feel the most emotional turmoil in the areas in which we are most resistant and scared, the places where we are most stuck or in denial about.

Usually, a dark moon (when the moon is pulling us deep into the inner depths of our emotions) or a full moon (when everything we try to hide from rises up) are the times when emotions feel most raw, exhaustion is real, life feels overwhelming and we just want to crawl under the duvet and hide. And one of the questions I am most frequently asked is: 'Why does the moon do this to me?'

The answer is that the moon doesn't do anything to us; she simply reflects back what is already within us to make us aware. And as the moon pulls on the tides of our emotions and illuminates our inner worlds, she helps us to see clearly which areas of our lives need our attention or where we are most stuck.

Once you start working with the moon's magic you will notice that the same recurring themes, emotions or reactions to the same person, issue or area of your life are evident over and over again, often in the same phase of the moon. It can feel a little like Groundhog Day at first, as the same lessons keep coming up, until you see them, face them and learn from them.

Emotions, like the tides, need to come and go. You need to allow yourself to experience them, let them show you what they need to show you, understand and process them – and then let them go.

The moon is like a universal signpost showing the way, and gently (or sometimes not so gently) nudging you back on track when you stray off. The rest is up to you. You can continue to be thrown around by your emotions, and life, or you can look to this ancient, mystical force to take back your power.

TAKING BACK POWER AND AWARENESS

Working with moon energy helps us to know ourselves like never before. She removes the masks we wear, uncovers the truth and takes us on a deep dive beneath the 'I'm fine' story we tell ourselves and others and into our hidden inner worlds – right to the heart of the matter. In short, the moon helps us look into our souls.

Month on month, as we journey with the moon, she helps to uncover our greatest fears, doubts and insecurities along-side our most hidden hopes, dreams and desires. She helps us to see what keeps us small and stuck and scared and also what our passion and purpose and unique individual gifts are – and what we are truly capable of when we claim our full potential and power.

With an increased awareness of what we suppress and hide (see previous section) comes empowerment – and a choice. We can choose to remain stuck in the same old patterns over and over again, suppressing and pushing down feelings or the voice of our deep inner knowing; or we can choose to face things and work with the phases of the moon to make the necessary changes.

Working with the moon helps us to take back control and accept responsibility for our own lives and feelings. As long as we tell ourselves that it's someone or something else's fault, we have to wait for that external situation to change before we can be happy. Once we take responsibility, however, we reclaim our power to make change and transform our lives.

You always have the power to create change. In every moon phase and every moment, you have a choice about what to do, how to react or act, what direction to take. It helps you to be aware of your triggers and, month on month, to be in flow with nature and life, rather than against it, working with your emotions and following your dreams. You'll start to notice your energy levels naturally start to drop near a dark moon, or that you are filled with the answers and insight you need around the first quarter; and you will learn to work with this natural rhythm and flow. You'll begin to realise that you are part of something much greater and that each and every one of us is connected.

The more you work with the moon, the more aware you will become of how you are affected in each of her phases, what the recurring emotions are signposting you to or which life areas need focus and attention. You'll know when you're starting to understand the moons cycles because as soon as you move out of alignment, you'll use the phases and energies of the moon to bring you right back on track.

RECONNECTION . . .

The moon is an incredible tool for reconnecting, not only back to your true self but also to life, nature and other people.

. . . to others

The moon brings us all together, which is a rare thing in our modern-day world.

Regardless of age, race, religion, orientation, beliefs, upbringing, wealth, status or even social-media following, we are all affected by the same energies and gravitational pull of the moon and we can all use her magic. Actually, although we do all experience the moon in the same phase on the same day, the northern and southern hemispheres will see the phases the opposite way round: the northern hemisphere will see the moon wax (grow bigger) from the right and wane (grow smaller) to the left, whereas the southern hemisphere will see her wax from the left and wane to the right.

One of the things I love most about Lunar Living, and the sisterhood in my online course is that they help us to know that we are never alone in how we are feeling. Back in ancient times, women would have gathered for a few days at a new moon to menstruate in a moon lodge or red tent. This would have been a sacred time of withdrawal from day-to-day life when women would share, support and encourage each other, and tune more deeply into the wisdom of the moon and their own heightened inner understanding and intuition during this time of the month. This kind of connection has sadly been forgotten in modern-day society, but it is invaluable, powerful and magical.

In a world where loneliness is so prevalent, Lunar Living brings people together. It is always so reassuring to see comments on my Moon Musings on social media, from people who share that they feel exactly the same. This coming together through shared emotions and experiences shows that we are not alone. The effects of each moon join us all as we begin to realise that others around us are being affected and feel the same way or are coming up against similar issues in comparable life areas. And in this way, Lunar Living – becoming aware of the moon's effects and phases – also helps us to deal with and support those around us much more effectively. We can be more understanding towards their emotional reactions around a new and full moon, and we become less likely to react back.

I remember being in central London on a full-moon day. There was a huge traffic jam as two cars met in the middle of the road and neither would reverse back and clear the way. Everyone was beeping their horns, shouting and swearing at each other, blaming, getting aggravated and arguing. I wanted them all to stop, and explain it was a full moon and that's why their energies and emotions were all heightened.

Now, imagine if just one of those drivers had understood this. Imagine if rather than acting out from that moon-fuelled emotional place of ego and 'I'm right', one of them had simply reversed. To take this further, imagine if they had then gone home that evening and, under the illumination of the moon, realised that they hadn't want to reverse because they felt like they were being pushed back in their job by their boss, and this was their subconscious way of taking a stand. Imagine if they'd then used the releasing power of the full moon to gently let go of the parts of them that didn't feel enough or felt small or pushed back and even perhaps started to realise that they also needed to release the job itself and move in a new direction. Imagine how much better the world would be if everyone understood Lunar Living!

. . . to nature

Working with Lunar Living also reconnects us back to the powerful cycle of nature, something else that is ever-more dismissed and forgotten in our man-made world. Yet, in truth, the energy that turns the tides, causes the leaves to fall from the trees, blossoms to grow and the seasons to change is the same life-force energy that moves through each and every one of us.

The moon and her phases affect so much of nature. Did you know that once a year, between October and December, there is a mass spawning of the corals on the Great Barrier Reef, influenced and triggered by the full moon? Or that the endangered seabirds the Barau's petrels all meet at the full moon to mate? And how about the Ephedra foeminea, a small flowerless plant that relies on pollinating insects and the moon for survival: every full moon, this plant produces pollen to attract flies and moths, which navigate using the light of the full moon. Or that some of your favourite wine may only taste so good because the moon's cycles have been taken into consideration when pruning, planning and bottling (there is also a strong theory that wine will even taste better when drunk on certain days in the lunar cycle).

In ancient cultures, all full moons were given names based on nature, as the full moons were used to track the seasons. This is where names like the wolf moon, the flower moon, the harvest moon and the cold moon come from.

All around us, nature moves with the moon and in seasons and spirals. Us humans are the only ones who feel we are not affected by nature's cycles, expecting that not only we, but also everything around us, should be the same every single day. But that's just not the way life is.

It is when we move out of alignment with nature and seasons and cycles that we become overloaded and stressed, eventually leading to suffering and burnout. By following and working with the ever-changing phases and cycles of the moon, Lunar Living helps you to reconnect back to nature – to rhythm and flow, seasons and cycles.

A COSMIC TIMER

Do you ever make it halfway through a year and wonder how you got to that point? I'll tell you how.

When we live life in a linear way, moving through every

day as though it should be the same, life passes us by. It has no meaning, rhythm or flow; instead, every day blends into the next with nothing to pause or break it up, except perhaps the weekend or an occasional holiday. We blink and we miss it – and before we know it, we are at the end of another year of unfulfilled dreams and goals. Nothing has changed.

Just as our ancestors had calendars based around the moon, we too can use this ancient cycle to keep ourselves in constant check and to ensure that we are always taking conscious control over the direction of our lives. Lunar Living helps you to keep showing up for yourself and your life, your purpose and your dreams.

How many times have you made a new year's resolution (or ten!), only to have lapsed by February and not even be able to remember what it was by May? Living a lunar life means that you will no longer throw a wish out there into the world and do nothing else about it, leaving it untended and forgotten about.

Lunar Living gives you an anchor – an intention to keep coming back to – and then a process to go through, over and over again, if necessary. Month on month, you set your intentions on the new moon, doing all you can to bring them to life during the waxing phase. The full moon is a time of completion and noticing what prevents or stands in the way. Then, during the waning moon, you work on releasing and letting go of obstacles or doubts, slightly changing direction if necessary, before infusing your intentions with more and more energy each new moon until they come to life.

The moon is a constant reminder to keep working on your dreams. You'll see just how much change you can create in 12 months when you begin to work with moon magic.

COMING HOME TO YOURSELF

I was writing this book during the Capricorn full-moon lunar eclipse in July 2019. On the night of the eclipse I went outside to find the moon, but couldn't see her anywhere. I paced the streets of London, getting more and more upset. 'I'm the Lunar Living "moon woman",' a voice inside me said. 'I talk to people about her all the time – I *have* to see the moon.' Then another voice said, 'Don't worry about seeing her. Just soak in the energies.' But the first voice grew louder. 'This isn't fair!' it cried. I even downloaded an app to try to track the moon in the sky as I walked the streets, muttering to myself about high-rise buildings and wanting to move to a secluded desert, so I could be with her all the time. Finally, I decided to give up. I told myself that I would meditate through the eclipse instead and that would be enough. So, I headed home, and just as I got to the top of my road (literally, I'm not kidding), there she was – in full eclipse mode. Waiting for me.

She simply wanted me to come home.

It brought me to tears. It felt like a powerful reminder that all we ever have to do is come back home. Back home to us. We spend so much time searching outside, metaphorically walking the streets to try to find what we are looking for. And it's there inside us, waiting all along.

That's what working with moon cycles is all about: coming home. It's about not being thrown around by life or emotions, feeling like it's not fair. Lunar Living gives you rhyme and reason, rhythm and flow, purpose and permission. It helps you to take back control of your life. Time after time, Lunar Living helps you to come back home to yourself.

YOUR LUNAR LIVING TOOL KIT

Throughout the book I refer to a number of techniques and strategies for working with the moon. For ease of reference, I've listed them here for you to consult as and when you need to.

✹ **Soul-vision board** A soul-vision board is a place where you collect pictures, images and representations of all of your dreams, desires, intentions – everything you want to create in your life. It can be on a big piece of card or even online, somewhere like Pinterest. Spend time looking at your board, as often as you can, to keep reminding yourself of the direction you are heading in, and how it might feel when you get there.

✹ **Intentions** An intention is a statement of clarity around your dreams. It declares exactly what you want in your life, and becomes the guiding force of your actions, words, choices, thoughts and beliefs, always helping to move you closer to what you want.

* **Affirmations** These are positive statements that you repeat to yourself over and over to reprogramme your thoughts, helping you to overcome doubts and fears and improve your self-belief. You'll find more on these on p. 187.

* **Visualisation** This is the act of using your imagination to see and feel your dreams and desires as though they are true in this moment. The more you can allow yourself to believe that you already have all that you desire in this moment, the easier it is to make it come true. See p. 189 for more on visualisation.

* **Gratitude practice** This is the practice of reflecting on all that you have to be grateful for. It is said that the fastest way to get what you want is to be grateful for what you already have. You can always find something to be grateful for.

* **Mirror work** Originally developed by the legendary motivational author Louise L. Hay, this is the daily act of looking at yourself in the mirror, often repeating positive affirmations, to help you to access your inner world.

✳ **Brain dump** This is the process of putting all of your thoughts and everything that comes into your mind down on paper.

✳ **Mind map** A mind map captures the thinking process that goes on in your head and helps you to turn it into creative ideas. You write the main idea or thought in the centre of a piece of paper and then continue to add subtopics, developing the theme as ideas come to you.

✳ **Shadow work** The shadow parts of you are usually unconscious until you become self-aware enough to start to notice and heal them. Here, you do the work of uncovering and accepting these parts of yourself – all those that you try to hide from or deny or consider to be weak.

✳ **Journaling** Taking pen to paper and writing down your thoughts, goals, affirmations, worries, whatever it may be, is a powerful and therapeutic practice for many.

Now we know what Lunar Living can bring into our lives, we can go on to look at the phases of the moon and how we can work with each one of them to take conscious control over our lives and create some of that moon magic!

A word on chakras

Just as the moon helps you to uncover your inner world of intuition, dreams and your soul, the chakras are the energy centres of your inner universe. Each one corresponds to a planet, bringing the energy of the solar system into your inner world:

- ✤ **Root chakra or muladhara (Mars)** – relates to your primal survival instincts
- ✤ **Sacral chakra or svadhisthana (Venus)** – relates to your emotions and desires
- ✤ **Solar plexus chakra or manipura (sun)** – relates to your personal power and ego
- ✤ **Heart chakra or anahata (moon)** – relates to all matters of the heart and love
- ✤ **Throat chakra or vishuddha (Mercury)** – relates to your communication in all forms
- ✤ **Third eye chakra or ajna (Saturn)** – relates to intuition and seeing things clearly
- ✤ **Crown chakra or sahasrara (Jupiter)** – relates to your connection to your higher self or soul

THE MAGIC OF THE MOON AND LUNAR LIVING

Moon magic made easy

Working with the magic of the moon and Lunar Living teaches us:

* self-care – showing us that there is a time to be and a time to do
* trust – in a guiding force and ancient wisdom and also in ourselves
* tuning into emotions – by allowing them to surface, so that we can become aware of them and what they are showing us
* taking back power – as we use the phases of the moon to create real change
* reconnecting – back to nature, others and a natural rhythm and cycle
* a cosmic timer – which helps us to stay accountable in making change and following dreams
* coming home to ourselves – month on month, the moon helps us to stop looking outside and turn our focus inwards.

CHAPTER 3:

Transform Your Life With the Phases of the Moon

'Trust in the moon, she whispers we'll be there soon'
'Guided by Waves' by Ash Radford

WORKING WITH MOON phases means that every month we have at least two opportunities to check in and see where we are in our lives – to create things that need to be created and release all that is standing in our way.

Journeying with the moon through her cycles helps us to work through similar cycles in our own lives. Using the moon's energies to release and let go allows us to create the space for new beginnings and amazing opportunities, ensuring that we continue to grow and move forward, rather than staying stuck in the past.

Working with the moon and her ever-changing phases also helps us to not fear change in life, as we come to see that everything is part of the same beautiful cycle, and that each part is as necessary as the last. We have to allow ourselves into darkness and surrender to be able to achieve fullness and light.

It's imperative that we play an active part in our own lives, that we hold ourselves accountable and take back our power. The moon gives us the tools we need; rather than waiting or leaving things to fate or being thrown around by our emotions or life circumstances or staying in the wrong job, relationship or situation for way too long, we can use these monthly opportunities and the magical energies of the moon to take back control of our lives and create real change, transformation and growth.

TAKE A DEEP, MOONLIGHT-FILLED BREATH

One of the simplest ways I find to explain the cycles, effects and energies of the moon throughout the month is by likening it to the breath:

* Sit back, close your eyes and take a big, full, deep breath in, pause for a moment at the top of the inhale and then take a big, full, deep breath out and pause for a moment at the bottom of the exhale.

* Take another deep breath in, pause. Then another deep breath out and pause.

* Repeat this a few times and really tune into and experience the cycle of the breath and how each phase makes you feel.

The dark moon is the lowest energetic part of the lunar cycle, and is just like the very bottom of your exhale – an empty space. Here, you feel as though you want to close your eyes and retreat inwards, be quiet and still. Even the body seems to close in and sink down as everything draws inwards, into this empty space. There is no energy for anything but simply being in that void and pausing, listening, resting.

As you begin to inhale, like the waxing moon, you feel an influx of energy. It's as though you literally begin to breathe life back into yourself. Your energy starts to return and, along with it, your inspiration and drive to go out there into the world and make things happen.

The full moon is the very top of your inhale. There is a sense of completion and fullness and everything feels alive and possible. Your whole being feels expansive, open and receptive. It's as though everything suddenly becomes clear.

As you exhale, like the waning moon, there is a feeling of release, surrender, letting go. As you get closer to the end of your exhale, everything seems to get more inwardly focused and quiet and small, returning back into the void.

Imagine for a moment what would happen if you remained at a certain part of the breath cycle for a long period of time. What would that feel like? Imagine always being at the top of your inhale – filled to bursting, hyper, anxious, overly energised; or, conversely, at the very bottom of your exhale – flat, lifeless, empty. This is, at times, how we live our lives: holding on, fearing change, getting stuck and allowing situations, expectations, fears, even other people to control and overwhelm us, or keep us small and empty.

Working with the cycles of the moon means that you will no longer allow this to happen. You will instead become so much more self-aware and keep yourself and your life in a constant flow.

So, with a deep breath in and out, let's look at the phases and how we can work with them in a little more detail.

EBB AND FLOW, WAX AND WANE

The moon is the feminine energy that connects us to our inner worlds, our emotions, our intuition, dreams and the call of our souls. Every month, she phases from dark to new, waxing to full, waning back to dark and, as she does, she takes us with her on a powerful inner journey. Each of the moon's phases brings its own opportunities and magic and takes us into different areas of our inner worlds to work with.

The two main phases many of us will generally work and weave magic with are the new and the full moon:

✴ The new moon is the time for renewal, new beginnings and starting over.

✴ The full moon is the time of completion, illumination and letting go.

As the moon moves between her phases she also waxes and wanes:

✤ The word waxing means growing or expanding, and it's during this phase that our energy grows with the moon; this is the creative part of the cycle.

✤ The word waning means shrinking or decreasing, and this is the releasing part of the cycle, as our energy levels get lower and more inward-focused.

In addition:

✤ The crescent phases are when the moon is less than half illuminated.

✤ The quarter moons are when we see half of the moon illuminated.

✤ The gibbous phases are when the moon is more than half illuminated.

As you begin to weave your own moon magic, you may wish to work with all of these phases or just simply with the magic of the full and new moons. Understanding how the different cycles affect you energetically is really useful and will further help you to work with and understand your own rhythms.

It is certainly worth a check-in at each turning point of the cycle, to make sure that you are moving in the direction you wish to head in and not straying too far off course. If you find yourself feeling particularly emotional, lost or coming up against any sticking points, check which phase the moon is in as this will give you more insight into why this could be happening, and help you to work with, rather than against, whatever is going on. You can also find which sign the moon is in at each phase and read up on that particular sign in Part II, 'The Moon in Each Zodiac Sign', to add a little extra moon magic.

Under each moon phase, I have given you some action points, and reflections from the moon. Use these as journal prompts (see p. 191 for more on journaling); write them at the top of the page and simply write what comes to you, allowing the wisdom and guidance of this moon to reflect back to you answers from within.

THE EIGHT PHASES OF THE MOON

There are eight official moon phases. I have started with the dark moon, as this is the end that creates a beginning, and sets the tone for the rest of the lunar month ahead.

As we've learned, the phases of the moon are not exact, and so cannot be divided into equal parts. I've tried to simplify the phases on the opposite page, but as a reference point, the moon spends around three and a half days in each phase. If you want to delve into working with each phase, you can use an online moon calendar for the exact days when the moon changes phase.

Note: there is a slight difference in the terminology used by astronomers and astrologers to describe some moon phases. I have used the astrological terms here.

1. The dark or balsamic moon
The dark moon begins 10/11 days after the full moon and takes us to the new moon.

2. The new moon
The new moon is the start of the lunar cycle and lasts around 3 days; it's two weeks to the full moon from here.

3. Waxing crescent moon
The waxing crescent moon begins 3 days after the new moon and lasts around 4 days.

4. Waxing first quarter
The first quarter moon begins 7 days after the new moon and lasts around 4 days; it's about a week until the full moon from here.

5. Waxing gibbous moon
The waxing gibbous moon begins 10/11 days after the new moon and takes us up to the full moon.

6. Full moon
The full moon arrives approximately 14/15 days after the new moon and lasts 3 days; it is two weeks to the new moon from here.

7. Waning gibbous moon
The disseminating moon begins 3/4 days after the full moon and lasts around 3 days.

8. Waning last quarter
The last quarter moon begins around 7 days after the full moon and lasts 4 days; it's about a week to the new moon from here.

Next, let's look at the phases in a little more detail.

The dark-moon into new-moon phase

Perhaps one of the most potent parts of the cycle, this is definitely a time to be honoured and turned into ritual – a time for self-care and self-enquiry. We ask people how they are on a daily basis, yet rarely stop to ask ourselves. This is the time to check in with ourselves and how we really are.

Working with the moon, particularly in her dark phase, gives you permission to rest, reflect, retreat and press pause – something that is so incredibly needed in our fast-paced society. This is a wonderful opportunity, every month, to catch up with yourself, to tune in and notice what comes up and to acknowledge your feelings and what they are trying to signpost you to.

This momentary pause helps you to get clear on where you are at. This can sometimes be a jarring reality check, but it is only from this present moment, right here, right now, that true and lasting change can happen. Quite simply, you can't know where you are going unless you know where you are.

From being realistic about where you are in this present moment you get to decide if this is still a path you wish to be on, a situation, relationship or job you wish to stay in. It becomes so clear under the dark moon whether or not you are in alignment with your heart and soul.

The dark moon time helps you to gain clarity and sets the theme for the rest of the month ahead, as you decide your way forward and what intentions you want to set under the new moon. You regain control of your life and begin to dream, to desire, to uncover what you want and to vision it into reality with the new moon. From here you begin to consciously choose the direction of your life.

1. THE DARK MOON

For me this truly is the ending that brings a new beginning. The dark-moon phase is the last few days of the waning moon, when she has waned so far that she is barely visible, yet still hasn't quite lined up with the sun, so isn't yet new. It is a time of endings, completing the cycle and preparing for the next one. This in-between void is a time of closure to help you to reset, release and not take anything into the next lunar cycle that you don't want or need. It is the most deeply healing part of the lunar cycle.

The days of the dark moon are the lowest energy point of the month, the most inward-facing, highly intuitive and emotional. You may find yourself exhausted around this time and yearning for solitude. If you have been pushing too hard, not taking care of yourself or giving away too much of your time and energy, you will especially feel this. This is your universal signpost to self-care.

The energy of the moon will literally pull you so far down that it forces you to stop, so that you can finally catch up with yourself and where you are, tune in and listen. Just as she disappears from the sky, the moon will take you into the shadowy inner realms of your emotions, subconscious and dreams, down into the depths of what you hide beneath the surface in day-to-day life.

The moon pulls you into the darkness so that you can see where you currently are in your life – like your own internal compass, showing you where you are stuck, travelling in the wrong direction or the dead end that you keep encountering. It shows you where you are out of alignment.

During these few days of the dark moon you may feel extremely emotional and 'dark' just like the moon, but rather than wallow in this, it is important to delve into what the emotion is there to tell you. Take some time to be with your emotions and to see which areas of your life they are most trying to signpost you to – these are the areas that need change and your attention over the coming month. It's during this dark moon phase that you choose to start over or change course slightly on things that are working, but need some extra focus, energy or love.

This time of the month may feel challenging as the darkness shows you all that you *don't* want, but this is simply so that you can begin to realise what it is that you *do* want.

Just as the moon is retreating from the sky, this is a few days out of each month where you must give yourself permission to do the same – to withdraw into yourself and take care of your own needs. Allow yourself time to integrate and process the lessons of the month just gone and to pause to prepare for the next lunar cycle. If you ignore the signals from your body, heart and soul to slow down, get quiet and rest at this time, you may find the month ahead filled with unnecessary challenges, exhaustion, burnout and a feeling of disconnection.

Use the darkness and inward focus of the moon to forge a deep connection with your emotions, intuition and inner knowing. This is not a time for 'doing'; that will come in a few days. For now, just delve into what is trying to get your attention and pause in the void where you can feel and listen and trust in what you are being shown.

The more you can honour this time, the more magic the rest of the month will hold, as you begin the cycle fully tuned in – to yourself and the magic of the moon.

Under the dark moon
❉ Take space from the outside world to self-care.
❉ Tune into and feel your inner world and emotions.
❉ Connect to your higher guidance and wisdom.

Reflections for the dark moon

❋ What feels most dark in my life right now?

❋ What emotions am I experiencing?

❋ What areas of my life are being most highlighted by
this dark moon?

2. THE NEW MOON

This is the day the moon catches up with the sun; when
the sun, the moon and the earth are all aligned in the sky.
It is the very beginning of a brand-new cycle and with it
the darkness starts to lift and the way forward becomes
clear. The arrival of the new moon may feel like a breath
of fresh air and life once more feels filled with possibilities
and opportunities.

This is where you continue the work from the dark moon
and use all of the wisdom you gained from being in the
darkness, from the deep emotion and soul searching. It's
time to take the discoveries you've made about what you
don't want and turn them into what you do want, acting on
the intuitive knowing that came to you in the dark-moon
phase. Believe in yourself and your hopes and dreams; the
new moon is like a blank canvas upon which you can create
anything you want. It allows you to visualise and imagine
all of your inner desires, goals, hopes and dreams and let
them surface. It's at this time that you can get the most
clarity on what you want in life and, most importantly, how
you can get there.

This is still not a 'doing' phase, but rather a time for making plans, preparing the ground and planting the seeds. It's where you get creative, get clear and set your intentions. You will find that your intuition and self-awareness are still heightened at a new moon and you are able to be clear and focused on what you want and need.

This is the beginning of your lunar adventure. Don't worry about the hows at this point – that will come later. For now, focus on what you want to create, manifest, achieve and bring to life in the month ahead. Unless you have a clear direction and focus now, other people, life, self-sabotage, habits and old ways of believing, thinking and doing will keep sending you back to the same place, again and again. The new moon gives you the opportunity to take conscious control over your life.

A word of warning, though: there may be resistance and hesitation around the new-moon time, especially if what you are about to create is something big and life-altering. If you are just starting out with living a lunar life, begin with small, manageable changes, rather than going for an immediate whole-life overhaul. And if the little voice of doubt does surface, listen and thank it – it's a sign you're on the edge of something epic!

Under the new moon

❋ Make a soul-vision board.

❋ Create some intentions and affirmations.

❋ Vision and dream your ideal life daily.

Reflections for the new moon

✹ What areas of my life need attention?

✹ What are my intentions for the next lunar cycle?

✹ What am I going to work on creating and manifesting and putting into motion?

Take a look at Part II (see p. 69) to read up on what it means when the moon is new in each zodiac sign; this will give you even more ways to work with this magic and guidance on life areas in which to create change.

The waxing phase

This is the part of the cycle that takes us from the new moon to the full moon, as the moon gets bigger and brighter in the sky every night. Many of us enjoy this phase; with its go-getter vibe, it's a get-things-done time.

This first half of the lunar cycle is much more external in nature, as we focus on the outer and the doing and putting into motion all that we can to make our new-moon dreams, intentions, goals and wishes come true. We use the growing illumination and rising energy of the moon to help us see things clearly and take action.

Our energy levels will grow with the waxing moon, alongside our motivation, inspiration and insights, bringing us all that we need to work towards our goals.

This is a wonderful time to develop a deep trust in the universe and life and the idea that you are being guided at all times. During the waxing phase, look out for signs, synchronicities, things falling into place perfectly, as if by magic. Notice too the nudges you get about things that aren't working, showing you that they are perhaps not for your greatest good.

As you tune more deeply into these signs, follow where they take you, and as you start to see results, you will begin to believe in yourself, your abilities and your inner knowing. This phase gives you all of the tools you need to chase your dreams; it's all out there waiting for you.

Use the growing light of the moon to be big, bold and brave. Get out there into the world just as the moon is doing. Shine and be seen.

3. WAXING CRESCENT MOON

This is when we see the first sliver of the moon in the sky – the time for action.

Just as the moon is beginning to grow and take shape, so are your new-moon intentions.

Now that you've committed to your new-moon visions and dreams, it's time to gather your resources, gain the knowledge, step up to the starting line and begin the work to make your seeds of intention bloom into life: nurture, feed and water them to give them the very best chance to grow.

It is under the crescent moon that you need to stay in alignment with your vision and goals and put into place all that you need to fulfil them. This moon phase can be a little tricky because, just as the moon in the sky is still only a sliver and far from full, your visions and goals may seem a long way from wholeness or completion. It may feel like there is a lot of 'doing' without seeing much in return. Creating what you want can seem daunting and stressful, especially if it's something new or important to you. Because of this it can be tempting to give up at the crescent moon and you need to be aware of excuses and inner doubts that can stand in your way.

Take care of yourself and your energy at this growing phase of the month; you're only at the very beginning. Find balance in the being and doing. Keep reminding yourself of your new-moon intentions and what they will bring into your life and stay true to your vision. Keep looking at your vision board too, saying your affirmations or doing the visualising (see p. 189) alongside taking action. Trust that your seeds have been planted and are starting to germinate beneath the earth, and that, just like the moon, the first signs of life are starting to show.

Start to take those first steps towards making your new-moon visions a reality. Stay strong, believe in yourself and seek help and support in getting your dream off the ground if you need it. The lunar journey has begun.

Under the waxing crescent moon

* Make a clear plan of how you will bring your
  new-moon visions to life.
* Keep repeating your intentions and affirmations.
* Spend time daily with your vision board or
  visualising in meditation.

Reflections for the waxing crescent moon

✴ What daily actions can I take towards my dreams?

✴ What inner doubts are surfacing for me right now?

✴ How can I find more trust in myself and my vision and dreams?

4. WAXING FIRST QUARTER

The moon is halfway towards full during the waxing first quarter and, as the name suggests, we're a quarter of the way through the lunar cycle.

As the moon continues to grow bigger in the sky, she brings energy, ideas, inspiration and everything you need to bring your hopes and dreams and ambitions to fruition; it's like the energy of the entire universe is on your side.

This is the time of the month you need to say yes to every invite you receive, notice every nudge from the universe and follow the synchronicities and signposts that will seem to appear daily: you think about someone and they call; you need something and it appears. Be open to everything around you, hear every conversation, open your eyes and see what's in front of you and be fully aware of the doors opening and pathways ahead that become clear. This is the time of the month to fully release yourself to the flow of life and allow the growing light of the moon to guide you to everything you need.

Your new-moon seeds of intention have now taken root. Be sure that you keep them as your reference point, so that you can take guided action rather than putting yourself into a tailspin and being thrown off course. The universe may send you a few curveballs at this point that require you to say no to certain things if they are not in alignment with your vision. Ensure that you are focused and committed to only giving your energy to your dreams.

You may find the voice of doubt, the not-good-enough and the imposter syndrome (the belief that your success is not deserved or a result of your own efforts or skills) begin to creep in around this phase of the lunar journey. You are so near, yet so far from completion, and doubts creep in for a reason: to check how much you really want your new-moon visions and wishes and what you are willing to do to realise them.

Remember too that it's ok to let go of outdated dreams and visions if they aren't serving you any more. But tune into your heart during this phase to work out whether they are genuinely no longer right for you, or if it's a fear-based diversion or self-sabotage tactic. If you do need to let go of something, wait for the waning cycle to do this; for now, simply take note of any inner doubts and fears. Recommit to your new-moon vision and use the growing energy of the moon to help bring you all you need to get there.

Under the waxing first quarter

- Be open to everything coming your way.
- Recommit to your vision and dreams and use them as a reference point.
- Watch out for the voice of doubt and/or imposter syndrome.

Reflections for the waxing first quarter

✤ Where is the growing light of the moon guiding me to right now?

✤ What do I need to say no to, to make more space for my vision?

✤ Is this doubt to show me I need to make a change or the voice of the imposter syndrome?

5. WAXING GIBBOUS MOON

Over the next few nights it will be hard to tell whether the moon is full or not as just a little edge will be missing.

Your energy levels will start to grow with this part of the lunar cycle. You're almost there – *so* almost there – but not quite. And, just like the moon you may feel that it's just that one little edge, that little something that is missing. There can be impatience around this time of the lunar journey – a frantic feeling of wanting to get things done but not being quite sure what or how. Be patient and trust that all the support you need surrounds you.

Many people find they don't sleep in the nights before the full moon. This is because the moon simply wants you to make it over the finish line. It's like she is whispering, 'C'mon, you have work to do, you don't have time to sleep. There are still dreams to make come true and goals to achieve.' The moon gives you extra energy now to help you to finish off all that you set out to do at the start of the month. This is the time to write through the night or dedicate all your time to finishing a project. Tune in deeply and see what is still left for you to do. It's the last big lunar push of energy to get things done.

As the moon illuminates more in the sky she may also begin to highlight where you are perhaps trying to open a door that isn't yours to open, or where you are still holding on to some of those outdated dreams you noticed under the waxing first quarter. Certain things may feel difficult or not quite be working to plan. Challenges can come along with this peaking energy to show you where adjustments need to be made, or perhaps where something needs a little more time or preparation or the release of certain obstacles that stand in the way. Don't try to do anything about any of this just yet; this is work for the waning last quarter, but take note of it all so that you are prepared.

This phase holds all the potential and power of your dreams. They are almost there. Notice where you have been procrastinating, not giving your dreams the required effort, or you have slipped out of good habits or fallen out of alignment with what you want. Under this phase it's also likely that what holds you back will come rushing to the surface so that you can be aware of it, so be mindful of the voice of doubt and doom. Fine-tune, dig a bit deeper, draw on the light and energy of the moon to get things done and remember it's not too late; you still have these last few days of the waxing moon to make a really big difference.

Under the waxing gibbous moon

🌟 Give that last big lunar push of energy to get things done.

🌟 Take note of challenges and difficulties.

🌟 Practise patience and trust.

Reflections for the waxing gibbous moon

🌟 What still needs to be done to take me towards my dreams?

🌟 What feels challenging or difficult right now?

🌟 How have I been procrastinating and not giving my dreams all they deserve?

6. FULL MOON

The moon is full in the sky. Once again, she and the sun have aligned, but this time on opposite sides of the earth, bringing opposing forces into play.

This is the peak energy time of the month – your energy is at its highest and, depending on whether you have been in your flow or fighting against it, you will either feel a moment of completion, or completely emotionally frazzled.

With the moon fully illuminated in the sky she shines down on your life so that you can see exactly how far you have come since the beginning of the cycle. This halfway point is a culmination: the time you either celebrate a goal that has been reached or see very clearly what has stood in the way of you getting to where you wanted.

If goals have been reached, celebrate them. Celebrate you and the effort you put in during the waxing part of the cycle to get to where you are. Give thanks for the abundance and magic in your life and show gratitude to anyone and anything that helped you reap the rewards of your new-moon seeds of intention.

Now is also the time to look at all the little nudges you may have received and things that seemed difficult during the waxing-moon phase. Notice where you strayed from your new-moon intentions, what you allowed to stop you or hold you back or where you let self-doubt, fears and self-sabotage and procrastination get in the way. Under the light of the moon you will be able to see things very clearly and this is a wonderful time to evaluate.

Perhaps it's that the intentions you set weren't something you wanted, after all. They were outdated dreams or influenced by other people or society's opinions. Maybe you can see clearly now that you didn't believe that you could achieve your new-moon wishes, and so you need to do some work around self-belief; or that your dreams and achieving them scare you, so you sabotage them. Use the illumination of the full moon to see what you need to see.

There can be a lot of emotion under a full moon. As the dark moon draws us inwards into our deep emotional centre, the full moon pulls all of our emotions up to the surface. Be very mindful of high emotion and conflict under a full moon. Be with and understand what your emotions are signposting you to, but save any action for the waning phase of the moon.

Alongside heightened emotion, you can feel frustration or

even anger around a full moon, usually aimed at all the lost opportunities, the chances you didn't take and the times you ignored the niggle of your intuition or didn't follow a sign. When you dig deeper it's often frustration at yourself, for staying hidden and small or for being pulled away from your new-moon intentions – for not allowing yourself to grow with the moon.

This is ok. It happens. But now, this is your golden moonlit opportunity to get very clear on what you need to release to move forward, so that this doesn't happen again. What stood in your way? Where did you sabotage and play small? What voice of self-doubt stopped you going after what you wanted? How did you ignore your gut feeling and the signs?

The full moon is when you get clear on and set in motion letting go of all that keeps you stuck. It is a time of forgiveness – of yourself and others – and a time to set the intention for what you want to let go of, release and end during the waning part of the cycle.

It may take many, many moon cycles for you to make the necessary changes or be ready to fully commit to releasing and letting go. Some lessons take time. Some new-moon wishes and intentions also take time to arrive, so use this full-moon time to check in with things that seem like they are on their way but may not be fully manifest yet and give them some full-moon creative energy and vibes.

Under the full moon

✦ Celebrate the success of anything that has come to completion.

✹ Get very clear on what has stood in your way or any course-correcting nudges you have received.

✹ Make a list of all that holds you back and what you want to release.

Reflections for the full moon

✹ What new-moon intentions, dreams and wishes have come true?

✹ What prevented me from achieving what I set out to achieve on the new moon?

✹ What do I need to let go of, release and end during the waning moon?

Take a look at Part II (see p. 69) to find out what it means when the moon is full in each zodiac sign. This will give you even more ways to work with this magic and guidance on life areas in which you want to create change.

The waning phase

This is the part of the cycle that takes us from the full moon back down to the dark moon, as she gets smaller and darker in the sky every night. Many people tend to skip this phase or forget to do the work in the second half of the cycle, but I implore you to do it as its effects are profound and make all the difference.

The potent power of this second part of the cycle comes from doing the work to release and heal what we came up against in the depth of the new moon and/or illumination of the full moon. As humans, we don't like change and we don't like to let go. We cling and we grip and we don't want to face up to big challenges. We feel and react to pain when it's present, then we forget to do the work to heal it or don't want to think about it when the intensity has dissipated. But unless we do the releasing and healing work, the same things will keep coming back up over and over again. So, be honest: are you dealing with the same issues and emotions time after time? Are you doing the work in the releasing part of the cycle – or ignoring it and hoping it goes away?

This is the part of the cycle where you let go of stories, fears and beliefs. It's when you do the deep inner work. As the waning moon draws your awareness in to your inner world, you release self-doubt, self-sabotage and voices of not enough. This phase helps you to focus on the changes you want to make in yourself and on the inside. It's like preparing the soil again, so conditions are ideal for planting once the new moon arrives again.

This phase also enables you to begin to release people, relationships, jobs, old agreements, people-pleasing, resentments, grudges, habits – anything and everything that holds you back. It's just as powerful as the waxing creation phase, as it is what paves the way for these creations to be able to take place.

7. WANING GIBBOUS MOON

The moon begins to lose a little of her fullness, night by night, as we move through the doorway from waxing to waning and begin our journey into the second half of the cycle.

Initially, after all the busyness and high energy in the run-up to the full moon, you may feel a slight dip in energy during this moon phase. It can be tempting to give up at this stage and simply wait for the new moon to come around again so that you can start over and make new or more wishes. Don't fall into this trap, as unless you release what stood in the way this time, the same things will come up in the next lunar cycle, and the next and the next.

Use the drawing-inwards energy of the waning moon to begin to process all that you have experienced through the cycle so far and learn from it. This is where you begin to finally understand all that has stood in your way and why – the fears and doubts that hold you back and what needs to change. It can be a time of great insight.

Instead of giving up the dream, take a step back. The moon is still bright in the sky, so use her illuminating light to get clear on your next steps: what worked? What didn't? And what needs to change? What do you need to let go of in order to move forwards?

This is also the phase for communication. If there are difficult conversations to be had to bring things to an end or people with whom you need to create some boundaries, now is the time. Plus, it's the time to share the insights and wisdom that have come to you through the cycle so far with others in your life who may be affected. It is a wonderful time of the cycle to be seen and heard.

This can also apply if you have a business (or an idea for one) and you still need to get your message out there into the world, so that your services can become known. Remember, this is not a time to start anything new, but to keep giving momentum to an existing goal or dream that you are bringing to life. You can also use this phase to gather any missing pieces of information or knowledge and to decide how you can make slight adjustments to do things differently in the next lunar cycle.

Under the waning gibbous moon

✴ Process all that you have experienced through the cycle so far and what it has taught you.

✴ Become aware of all that has held you back from achieving your new-moon intentions.

✴ Broach any difficult conversations and share what you have learned and any changes you intend to make.

Reflections for the waning gibbous moon

✴ What wisdom and insight have I gained through the cycle so far?

✴ How can I begin to shed, release and surrender?

✴ Who do I most need to communicate my feelings to and why?

8. WANING LAST QUARTER

The moon is halfway towards new during the waning last quarter, and as the name suggests, we're three quarters of the way through the lunar cycle.

As the moon wanes and gets smaller, her energy is encouraging and supporting you to surrender and let go, let go, let go – just as she is doing. The moon shows, in perfect simplicity, that the only way to make room for new beginnings is by letting go of all that holds you back.

There may be a feeling of uneasiness around this phase of the lunar cycle as you feel change coming and perhaps a sense of things 'slipping away'. Drawing upon what you have learned through the cycle so far, this phase is where you do the real work of releasing what does not help or serve you in any way. This is really important, as otherwise it will come up again during the next cycle. Remember that some things may take a while to release, just as they take time to manifest. But the more times you become aware of them and lean into surrender, the more overall change you make.

This applies to the inner work around your self-doubt and self-belief, outdated narratives and stories and fears. Also, the outer work of shedding situations, people, environments, setting boundaries and getting clear on when to say yes and no in future. Affirmations, mirror work and journaling (see p. 28) can all be powerful here.

At this crossroads in the cycle, where the moon is once again half lit in the sky, look back over your journey so far and forward to where you still want to go. Give a last push to wrapping things up and making any necessary changes. Do all the things you have been putting off, get organised and prioritise.

As this is a halfway point between the full and new moon you may find things finally coming together, or that problems, mistakes or whatever you have been avoiding catch up with you now. This is a pivotal moment in the cycle. Take responsibility, face up to things and, if necessary, decide to let go of certain things for good, or find a new approach towards your goals and dreams that you can implement during the next lunar cycle.

Your energy will begin to get quieter and more inwardly directed, your intuition stronger and your tolerance for dealing with anything that is not right for you will become much less as you make your way, once again, to the dark-moon phase. And the cycle begins all over again . . .

Under the waning last quarter moon
* Make a last effort to finish things off, wrap things up and do what you have been putting off.
* Take inspiration from the moon and do daily work around letting go.
* Take responsibility, face up to things and make decisions for your future.

Reflections for the waning last quarter moon
* What do I need to finish up, complete or end?
* What decisions do I need to make about my future?
* What am I not ready to release just yet?

Moon magic made easy

In all the work I do and in all areas of my life, I like to try to keep things as simple as possible to ensure that I actually do what I need to do, and don't find a million excuses not to! Life is already busy enough without adding unnecessary pressure.

So, it is better to honour and genuinely work with a few of the phases than try to work with all of them and not have the time to give this magic-making the attention it deserves.

To keep things simple:

* **The new moon** will help you to decide what you want to create in your life and move forward into new beginnings.
* As the moon **waxes** (grows bigger), do all that you can to bring your vision and goals to the forefront of your life. Work with the growing energy of the moon to get out there into the world, say yes, notice the synchronicities and signs and follow the light of the moon wherever it takes you.
* **The full moon** will bring completion and illuminate your life as it is, to help you see what stands in your way and needs releasing.
* As the moon **wanes** (gets smaller), use her releasing energy to shed, release, surrender and let go of situations, people, habits, outdated beliefs, sabotage tactics and anything else that stands in your way.

CHAPTER 4:

Zodiac, Moon and Sun Signs

HERE IS WHERE working with the magic of the moon really begins to take shape. The moon moves between each of the 12 signs of the zodiac every two to two and a half days, passing through all of them within a lunar month. This means she falls in a different sign of the zodiac every full and new moon through the year, bringing the story, energy and magic of each sign into focus for us to work with. We will all be affected by this, regardless of our individual signs.

Each zodiac sign brings different influences, lessons, opportunities, challenges, positive and testing aspects, traits and a different focus and life area into the moonlight. This helps us to keep flowing with the rhythm of life as we use the different energies, characteristics and symbols of each sign to help us to explore, heal and delve deeper into the relevant areas in our own lives.

As a general guide, the watery signs take us into our emotional realms, the earth signs into grounding and facing reality, the fire signs bring passion and enthusiasm and the air signs help us to dream and vision:

Water – Cancer, Scorpio, Pisces
Earth – Taurus, Virgo, Capricorn
Fire – Aries, Leo and Sagittarius
Air – Gemini, Libra, Aquarius

Remember that the new moon will always be in the same sign as the zodiac season that we are in (as the sun and the moon are aligned in the sky – see p. 50), and so all of the aspects of this sign will come into play. The full moon will always be in the sign opposite to the current sun sign (as the moon is on the opposite side of the earth to the sun), which brings the opposing forces of the two signs into action.

We then have cardinal, fixed and mutable signs. The simplest way to think about these is that cardinal signs are the leaders and begin things, fixed signs 'fix' or stabilise things and the mutable signs bring transition and change. So every season will start with a cardinal sign, have a fixed sign in its middle and end with a mutable sign, once again giving us a cycle and flow to work with.

Cardinal – Aries, Cancer, Libra, Capricorn
Fixed – Taurus, Leo, Scorpio, Aquarius
Mutable – Gemini, Virgo, Sagittarius, Pisces

This means, for example, that Aries will start spring, Taurus will stabilise things for us in the middle of the season and Gemini will start to prepare us for the transition into summer and so on.

Very often, we are all encountering the moon chaos together, with everyone having similar experiences. But every once in a while, you may find certain moons where everyone around you seems to be in the depths of despair and emotion and you feel as though you are flying high and everything is falling into place. This is because each moon and the sign she is in brings up its own individual life lessons and guidance. If you have already done the inner work and are living by what this moon is calling you to work on, you'll feel an amplified energy as this moon propels you further along your path. If, however, this moon is bringing up a life lesson or an area that you are avoiding, in denial about or hiding from, you will feel this extremely strongly as the moon tries to show you the truth of the matter and bring it to the surface.

I'm also asked a lot whether you will feel a moon more strongly when it is full or new in your zodiac sign and the answer is yes. This is because it is 'your' moon, and so acts like your biggest cheerleader. It gives you further support and encouragement to help you to grow and move forward in whatever is being offered under your sign, and sometimes these lessons are the hardest to learn. This will apply whether the moon is in your sun or moon sign.

Your sun sign is the one that the sun was in when you were born, and is the aspect of astrology or horoscopes that most people are familiar with; it tends to give you a glimpse into certain personality traits, life attitudes and behaviours that you may exhibit.

Your moon sign is based on the position of the moon at

the time of your birth, and tends to give you more insight into your inner world of emotions, dreams, intuition and your soul. I know for me personally, finding out my moon sign was a game changer, as there were certain aspects of my star sign that didn't resonate with me, but it all made so much sense when I found out my moon sign. There are plenty of online calculators which will help you to find out your moon sign, but as the moon moves through the signs every few days you need to know the exact time of your birth to be certain of it.

Now, get ready for Part II, where we will take a closer look at the moon in each zodiac sign and see what lessons, wisdom and guidance she is offering us as she moves through them.

Moon magic made easy

✳ The moon moves between each zodiac sign every two to two and a half days, passing through the whole of the zodiac within a lunar month.

✳ The new moon will always fall in the same zodiac sign as the sun, as the sun and the moon are aligned in the sky.

✳ The full moon will always be in the opposite sign, as the moon is on the opposite side of the earth to the sun.

✳ The energy around you, the way you feel, the life areas brought into focus, the lessons and guidance offered by the moon will be affected by which sign the moon falls when she is new/full.

✳ You will usually be more affected by the pull of the moon when she is new or full in your sun/moon sign and also if it brings into focus areas of your life that need work or attention.

PART II:

The Moon in Each Zodiac Sign

CHAPTER 5:

The Moon in Aries

The moon to be brave and bold

Element: *Fire*
Quality: *Cardinal*
Ruling planet: *Mars, the planet of war*
Symbol: *The Ram*

BIG, BOLD, FIERY and full-power – the Aries moon brings with it immense energy, which will either feel incredibly positive or hugely emotional, depending on what is happening in your life.

MY MOON MUSINGS

If you are moon-sensitive, this moon can feel quite intense, irrational, impulsive or restless, or there may be a feeling of heightened energy and a frenzy of excitement in the air. Adding fuel to the fire is a good way to describe this moon, as whatever you are currently going through will be intensified. If there is a burning, deep desire to create change in your life and start something new, such as a new career, relationship or direction in life, or to take an adventure and travel to somewhere you have never been, this will be amplified and you will suddenly have the courage, agency and tools to make it happen.

On the other hand, you may feel impatient and frustrated, especially if you are being held back, unclear on your direction or ignoring your soul's calling. The Aries moon will magnify this, and you may find yourself short-tempered and overwhelmed. Notice to whom and at what your frustrations are directed, as this may give you a clearer idea of what you are avoiding or when you are not listening to what needs to change.

Aries, being the first sign of the zodiac and a cardinal sign, deals with primal new beginnings and needs. It will help you become the leading role in your own life, releasing all that's in the way. As such, this moon can bring a demanding energy of 'I want what I want and I want it now', and so you may find yourself acting from impulse and ego. Try instead to tune in a little deeper to the inner yearnings of your heart and soul to get in touch with what you *truly* want. It can sometimes take time and practice to learn the difference between the wants of the ego and the soul, but as a guide, the voice of the ego tends to be loud, demanding and almost childlike, while the voice of the soul is quiet, calm and certain – literally, like a wise old soul.

The trick to this moon is to get very clear on what your deep soul calling is, as opposed to what comes from the ego, what society says, conditioning or fear. Once you can get clear on the true calling of your soul and whispers of your heart, there could not be a better moon under which to align to your deepest guidance, wisdom, truth and purpose in life.

If you choose to listen and, most of all, 'feel', you can really discover things about yourself under this moon. Aries urges you to give up the doubts and the back and forth between what you 'should' do and what you truly want to do. Under an Aries moon you can gain huge clarity on emotions, beliefs, relationships, identities and anything that you need to let go of. It's a moon of deep inner healing, allowing old wounds to surface, stuck stagnant energy to shift and anything holding you back to be released.

It will also bring a huge surge of passion, inspiration and motivation to move forward – to get things done, to finish long-abandoned projects or pick back up dreams and ideas that the little voice of doom and 'not good enough' managed to convince you not to follow. This moon will help you to propel yourself forward: it's the Aries ram locking its sights (and horns) on the direction you want to head in and not allowing anything to stand in the way.

If you are deliberately avoiding new beginnings and have known for a while that changes need to be made but have been disregarding the inner voice, Aries may literally 'ram' you into action. This is the perfect time for being spontaneous and taking risks, following your instincts, impulses and intuition and using this fiery energy to help you see past the nagging voice of doubt, instead believing in yourself and your deepest passions and calling.

Aries will help you to be assertive, put yourself first, shamelessly self-promote and to shine as brightly as the moon in the sky. Allow the headstrong ram to help you take charge of your life, boldly step into action and fearlessly ask for what you need. Be brave and take the first steps towards something that has been scaring you, or you have been putting off. This is a moon for action and taking a leap of faith.

THE ARIES MOON CALLS YOU INTO . . .

. . . putting yourself first and following your own path. It lights your inner fire and the dynamic, courageous energy it brings helps to burn through all that keeps you stuck, to ram through your constraints and to push you into your individual greatness and real purpose on this earth. Aries will help you to take the first steps towards believing in yourself and telling the world all about it.

MARS, THE GOD OF WAR, RULES ARIES

Mars represents your basic energy, your survival needs and your root chakra (see p. 30). What is the primal, instinctive idea or dream coming up for you over and over again, but which you suppress with the grown-up voice and all the reasons you – supposedly – can't make it work? What do you have a real passion for in life? Mars will bring up all the fears (for survival) that you allow to control your life and hold you back as the ego tries to 'protect' you. On the other hand, Mars also uses the same energies to propel you forward to achieve, if you are brave enough and to follow your purpose and live to your full potential. Excitement and fear feel exactly the same in the body, and so in all moments you have a choice: are you going to use this feeling to hold you back or to propel you towards fulfilling your potential.

NEW MOON IN ARIES – FALLS IN ARIES SEASON BETWEEN 21 MARCH AND 19 APRIL

Aries season marks the beginning of the astrological new year, the start of spring and the spring equinox, and this new moon marks new beginnings. The traditional new year has never resonated with me; I've always found it hard to wish and dream and vision when it's bleak and dark and cold in January. So, this has always marked a real time of new beginnings for me – with new growth and life – and I hope it will for you too.

Use this fiery new moon of action and energy to 'start over', especially if you don't feel that the year has quite brought you all that you hoped for. It's your second big chance of the year to make a change – like hitting the refresh button.

Use the Aries new moon to . . .

✤ . . . take charge of your life. Make a 12-month plan of what you want this astrological year to bring you; get clear and focused and make deadlines and commitments.

✴ **. . . get clear on your soul calling and purpose.**
Make a list of all the things you are good at and love
doing.

✴ **. . . put yourself first**. Promise one way you will put
yourself first every day during the waxing moon; this
may be as simple as ten minutes dedicated just to
you each morning.

FULL MOON IN ARIES – FALLS IN LIBRA SEASON
BETWEEN 23 SEPTEMBER AND 22 OCTOBER

This is the first full moon following the autumn equinox.
It's a time of inner harvest, so look back at the intentions
you set at the spring equinox or start of the zodiac or traditional new year, and allow this bright, bold full moon to
illuminate what has stopped you achieving them. It's time
to let go of all the limitations you put on yourself, the sabo-
taging fears and beliefs, the expectations, the stories you hide
behind, the blockages and barriers.

Many people find they can't sleep under this full moon
and so if you find yourself restless and wide awake, you are
truly being called to action. What is it that you are not
fulfilling? What inner calls are you ignoring through fear or
doubt? How are you not following your passions and
purpose? You know deep down what it is that you should
be doing, and, if you are really honest with yourself, the
reason why you are not.

The sun is in Libra during this full moon so the themes

of Libra, such as relationships, finding balance, self-care and tuning into the wisdom of your heart will now be highlighted by this full moon with Aries energy added to them.

If you find this moon takes you into heightened emotional states, make sure that you allow time for self-care (see p. 12). In all decisions you make under this moon be sure that you are not acting from rash, fiery ego energy and instead check in with your heart. Relationships may also once again come under the moonlight, with the full-moon energy helping you to finally make changes, set firm boundaries and release behaviours and even relationships.

Use the Aries full moon to . . .

✹ . . . **gain clarity on what needs to go from your life once and for all**. List three things that always seem to hold you back that you can work on releasing from your life through the waning-moon phase.

✹ . . . **shamelessly self-promote and share your greatness and gifts with the world**. In front of the mirror repeat daily, 'I believe in myself', as you look yourself in the eyes and decide on one way you can share your talent, gifts and message out into the world.

✹ . . . **take action towards something that has been scaring you, or you have been putting off**. Identify one action you will commit to taking during the waning-moon phase, and one thing you can do each day to take you closer to this. Make an action plan.

The keywords for Aries are 'I AM'

Use this as a journal prompt and see what flows to you in answer. Set some intentions or create some affirmations (see p. 187) using this declaration at the beginning – things like:

✴ I AM brave and bold.
✴ I AM on purpose.
✴ I AM bringing my dreams to life.

What to watch out for under an Aries moon:

1 Self-confidence that verges on arrogance and being too self-centred.

2 Temper tantrums, especially if you feel someone is questioning your life direction (or lack of).

3 Becoming too competitive and ruthless in getting what you want.

 A crystal for this moon: moonstone or moss agate for new beginnings, celestite to hear your soul's wisdom or bloodstone for bravery and motivation

CHAPTER 6:

The Moon in Taurus

The moon to be grounded and real

Element: *Earth*
Quality: *Fixed*
Ruling planet: *Venus, the planet of love*
Symbol: *The Bull*

THE FIRST EARTH sign of the zodiac, the Taurus moon is all about dealing with what is real, deep roots, security and stability and feeling at home in you. As such, it may have you going to ground.

MY MOON MUSINGS

Root to rise is the essence of this moon. You need to be rooted in your own reality, your own truth and to know, accept and own every part of yourself completely, wholeheartedly and unapologetically – which, first and foremost, means reaching into your depths and seeing yourself for who you truly are.

This moon will show you the reality of your life as it is

right here, right now – the truth, the whole truth and nothing but the truth. It's only from this point of being in the reality of the present moment that necessary change can ensue. It's a moon for focusing your intention on what matters to you and what needs to change in order for you to become completely happy and secure.

This moon will help you to build a safe sanctuary in all aspects of your life from the emotional to the financial, and in doing so you may feel some foundations start to shift and some restructuring take place. This can feel quite scary, as Taurus doesn't like initial change, and you may notice your-self trying to cling on tightly, feeling unbalanced, ungrounded, unsure or overly emotional. Notice what you are trying to cling on to and why – often it is because you have created a false sense of security out of this particular thing, and Taurus only wants what is genuine and lasting to remain.

That's why this moon may have you feeling like a bull in a china shop, as structures that aren't working start to fall down and anything that isn't built upon a real, dependable, true foundation crumbles. Try to trust in this whole process, as the security this moon is asking you to find is something deeper – it's a security and belief in yourself and your future, based on being firmly rooted in your own truth and reality.

As the Taurus moon deals with practical matters of mater-ial security it makes this a wonderful moon to welcome in financial abundance. Take some time to go through your finances and get to grips with them; notice any stories you have around money concerning lack and instead be open to welcoming in abundance, and receiving alternative or new avenues of income, and figuring out ways you can use your passions to help make you money.

Taurus also helps you to understand that true security, stability and, ultimately, happiness come from the inside. Sometimes we can use the material and outside world to fill a void on the inside, but material gains should be complementary to rather than the reason for your happiness. Taurus wants you to create a life in which your happiness is an inside job and you feel whole, complete, safe and secure in yourself.

Mostly though, this is a moon for self-care. It's a moon that wants to know what brings you pleasure and joy and fills you up. It teaches you about enjoying life. Rather than adopting the masculine energy of doing, this moon shows you what gifts are available to you if you are willing to slow down and tune in to the feminine energy of receiving. This is a moon of focusing more on the inner journey than the outer, of fertilising your own earth, your heart and your soul, so that your own seeds can take root and flourish.

THE TAURUS MOON CALLS YOU INTO . . .

. . . finding a deep inner security that only comes from feeling safe and fully at home in you. It's a moon of allowing yourself to be guided by your own wisdom, and realising that when you stop pushing and pulling, life becomes easy and pleasurable. It's a moon of giving yourself exactly what you need when you need it, and it's a time for a life review:

finding balance, making vital changes for your security and, most of all, finding your roots – the things and people that nourish, sustain, nurture, feed, inspire, hold you up and bring you absolute joy.

VENUS, THE PLANET OF LOVE, RULES TAURUS

Venus brings out the self-care element of this moon, asking you to love yourself and the body you are in. It's a wonderful moon to notice if you resist self-care. Do you feel it's selfish? Lazy? Do you feel you are not deserving of your own love and care? Do you struggle to treat yourself? Do you never allow yourself to slow down and rest? These are all ways in which you sabotage the universal flow of energy and receiving, but this moon will help you to see this and make amends, so that you can fully receive in order to be able to give.

NEW MOON IN TAURUS – FALLS IN TAURUS SEASON BETWEEN 20 APRIL AND 20 MAY

This new moon is here to help you to slow down and make things a reality. You may feel a real sense of exhaustion and lethargy under this moon as the Taurus dark-moon energy literally forces you into taking it easy, so that you can listen to the voice of your intuition and make necessary changes.

You will feel the dark pull of this moon, particularly if you hide behind 'busyness'. This moon will show you very clearly all the talk but no action, all the dreaming but never achieving.

You see, we use 'being busy' as an excuse not to delve deeper, to really listen to what is going on and, often, as an avoidance tactic for why we 'can't' focus on ourselves or our dreams and inner desires.

New moons are usually a time for new beginnings, but this is not one in which to make any hasty decisions. Instead, be here now, in this moment, this breath, this emotion. Hunker down and take care of yourself. Slow down and allow things to unfold and emerge just as they should. Be kind and gentle and with yourself – spend a lot of time in nature, take long walks, go barefoot on the earth, eat nourishing foods, get a massage, sink into a bubble bath, spring clean your home and do anything and everything that brings you pleasure and joy.

Use the Taurus new moon to . . .

* **. . . self-care, self-care, self-care.** Make a list of at least three things that you can do over the Taurus new-moon period that are just for you. Notice how you feel about self-care, and if it's something that's hard for you to implement, try just one act of self-care every day under the waxing moon.

* **. . . assess where you are.** Use this earth energy to stop, pause, reassess, balance and ground. Take a look at how far you have come, where you are right now

and whether you are moving in the right direction. Bring yourself back into a place of being grounded in the here and now.

✱ **... slow down.** Slow right down and spend time being present and completely in the moment. Take a digital detox, even just for a few hours, turning off all communication with the outside world so that you can travel inwards.

FULL MOON IN TAURUS – FALLS IN SCORPIO SEASON BETWEEN 23 OCTOBER AND 21 NOVEMBER

This full moon wants you to get right into the dirt, into the earth, to whatever you bury. It's going to stir up and bring to the surface who and what triggers you at your deepest level. It's going to shine a full-moon light on your deepest insecurities and all the things you allow to go unsaid and unheard. Everything you push below the surface is going to come back up. But only so you can see it, feel it, learn from it, heal it and rise from it.

It's a moon for appreciating the blessings and learning from the burdens, turning your so-called weaknesses into strengths, your challenges into golden opportunities and for focusing on creating instead of resisting and being bull-headed.

The sun is in Scorpio during this full moon, so the themes of Scorpio – such as vulnerability, intensity and deep inner emotion – will now be highlighted by this full moon with Taurus energy added to them.

The combination of these two zodiac signs can be quite transformative. Remember that we are only ever able to be truly vulnerable when we feel safe and secure, and Taurus brings this dependable safe space. It's a wonderful moon to allow your shadows to surface, as Taurus will help you to love, accept, own and embrace them, so that your light can shine even brighter, taking you towards the lasting safety and security that come from within.

Use the Taurus full moon to . . .

❋ . . . **do an emotional cleanse**. Let go of old emotions that you no longer need such as blame, resentment, shame. Make a list of anything that has been holding you down or keeping you stuck this year and use the waning moon to release it.

❋ . . . **feel at home in you**. Use the combination of these two zodiac signs to fully accept both your light and shadows. How can you love and accept yourself more? Create some affirmations (see p. 187) to help release your fears around the vulnerable parts of you.

❋ . . . **create lasting foundations.** As the full moon shines a light on your life, which foundations feel wobbly or unstable? Begin to let some of these go over the waning moon, so that you start to find firmer ones.

The keywords for Taurus are 'I HAVE'

Use this as a journal prompt and see what flows to you in answer. Set some intentions or create some affirmations (see p. 187) using this declaration at the beginning – things like:

🌟 I HAVE safe structures in my life.
🌟 I HAVE time to self-care.
🌟 I HAVE a trust in myself; I feel at home.

What to watch out for under a Taurus moon:

1 Becoming overly materialistic, looking to the material world for answers and security.

2 Aversion to change, so much so that you would rather stay in unhappy situations and make excuses for them.

3 Being stubborn – so incredibly stubborn.

 A crystal for this moon: citrine for financial abundance, black tourmaline for grounding and security or rose quartz for self-love and care

CHAPTER 7:

The Moon in Gemini

The moon to be inspired and create change

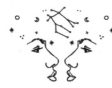

Element: *Air*
Quality: *Mutable*
Ruling planet: *Mercury, the planet of communication*
Symbol: *The Twins*

OUTGOING, LIVELY AND inquisitive, the Gemini moon brings an influx of inspiration and much-needed change.

MY MOON MUSINGS

This moon may have you feeling like there are two (or more) people living inside your head. You will flit from one thought and emotion to another in a matter of minutes and each one will feel so real. It's yes, it's no, it's this, it's that, you're staying, you're going, it's right, it's wrong . . . The uncertainty and indecision or even just the noise in your head can make this a confusing time.

As this is an airy moon, you may find yourself in your

head a lot. The Gemini flip switch will cause you to start questioning absolutely everything, particularly why you have allowed yourself to stay in certain situations or stuck in the same doubts and fears and old emotions for so long.

But the element of confusion under this moon has a real purpose. It is asking you to find the real truth of the matter – to move away from what is expected of you, to let go of ways of thinking, beliefs and choices that have not been working for you and may even be holding you back.

It's a moon that wants you to step into your truest authenticity and share your unique gifts and talents with the world. As such, this moon brings with it a lot of ideas, downloads of inspiration, a to-do list, a need to expand on your knowledge, learn more, gather more, make more connections, go out into the world more, do more, become more and share more.

Which brings us to one issue that can arise under this moon: the 'jack-of-all-trades, master-of-none' energy – the energy of starting a hundred tasks but not completing any, or coming up with ten brilliant ways to move forward in life, but acting on none.

Some of you will also use this as a form of self-sabotage, becoming so overwhelmed by the sheer number of ideas that come to you that you feel inadequate or afraid, so you run and hide. Be wary of this. Write down everything that comes to you. Brain dump it. Mind map it. (See p. 29.) But don't let any of it pass. Because in among the numerous ideas and light-bulb moments you will have under this moon, there will be nuggets of gold that will help you to get to where you really want to be.

With the sign of the twins you may find your dark and your light, your head and your heart, your courage and your fears, your dreams and your sabotage, your truth and your lies, your self-belief and self-doubt, your intuitive introvert and your expressive extrovert all fighting for attention. Part of you wants to be open and communicative, the other part wants to hide away. Part of you wants to run out into the world shouting, 'Finally, here I AM!', but the other half is saying, 'Ohhhh no, not me. Who am I? I'm not good enough/clever enough . . . ' (insert self-limiting belief as applicable).

There is a beautiful Native American parable that helps explain this perfectly:

An old Cherokee was teaching his grandson about life. 'A fight is going on inside me,' he said to the boy. 'It is a terrible fight and it is between two wolves. One is evil – he is anger, envy, sorrow, regret, greed, arrogance, self-pity, guilt, resentment, inferiority, lies, false pride, superiority and ego.'

He continued, 'The other is good – he is joy, peace, love, hope, serenity, humility, kindness, benevolence, empathy, generosity, truth, compassion and faith. The same fight is going on inside you – and inside every other person, too.'

The grandson thought about it for a minute, then asked his grandfather, 'Which wolf will win?'

The old Cherokee replied simply, 'The one you feed.'

Under this moon you need to decide which twin/wolf to feed: if you feed doubts and fears, they will always hold you back; so you must feed self-belief, gratitude, ideas and opportunities to ensure that they keep coming.

THE GEMINI MOON CALLS YOU INTO . . .

. . . making change. One thing that Gemini loves is change. Gemini struggles with trusting emotions and instead wants it all to be practical, rational and logical. So under this moon you will find that a lot of raw emotion dissipates (you may even feel a total disconnect with your emotions) and this can be helpful in allowing you to problem solve and figure out exactly where you are in life, where you want to go and how to get there. The twin mirror will help you to see all sides of any situation you are still ruminating over and perhaps the bigger-picture vision to see why what happened has happened so that you can move on. Gemini doesn't like to stay stuck in the past and will bring an optimism to encourage you to move forward.

MERCURY, THE PLANET OF COMMUNICATION, RULES GEMINI

Gemini is a great communicator and this moon is a good time to have any difficult conversations. Gemini will help you to speak your mind and your truth. Ruled by the master messenger Mercury, Gemini wants you to spread your unique individual message out into the world, so allow all your needs and desires to be fully seen and heard under this moon.

Express yourself, speak your truth with clarity, get curious, open your mind, expand your horizons and seek out the new opportunities coming your way.

NEW MOON IN GEMINI – FALLS IN GEMINI SEASON BETWEEN 21 MAY AND 20 JUNE

This can feel like a moon of more, more, more, and it can be a bit conflicting. New moons usually call us into stillness and renewal, while this one is busy and extroverted. But that's where its gifts lie. This moon helps you get things done, start over and find new beginnings, with change-loving Gemini to help you move forward. Use the energy of this moon to map your way forward, as it will be clear like never before.

This new moon encourages you to go out there into the world, make connections, gather information, learn, grow, share. It's a moon of communication, helping you find the people 'in the know', to be in the right places at the right times and to come across the information you need. Watch out for the signs and little nudges, follow your instincts and listen to your intuition – they will all be high under this new moon.

Use the Gemini new moon to . . .

✷ . . . discover your unique individual message. Use this as a journal prompt under the new moon and allow the answers that come to you to set your new-moon intentions and guide your way forward through the waxing moon.

✹ . . . **gain new ideas and inspiration**. Create a mind map or brain dump (see p. 29) all the ideas that come to you; there will be some gems in there that you can focus on in the waxing moon.

✹ . . . **follow your intuition**. Make a list of the information, people, knowledge and anything you would like to gain or receive over the waxing moon, then follow your intuitive nudges.

FULL MOON IN GEMINI – FALLS IN SAGITTARIUS SEASON BETWEEN 22 NOVEMBER AND 21 DECEMBER

Unsettling, confusing, restless and curious are just a few of the words to describe the strong energy of this full moon. You may also find that you have crazy dreams running up to it.

There can be a nervous energy about this moon, as you flit from one thing to the next, and so anxiety levels can be high. You may talk to yourself a lot, with a constant narrative in your head about everything, questioning yourself: 'Why do I do this/think like this/say that?' etc. There is a lot of power in this if you use it as a form of self-enquiry rather than self-punishment.

Use the light of this full moon and the Gemini twin mirror to allow things to surface, and to look at yourself and your fears and self-limiting beliefs. If you find yourself stuck in the same patterns/situations over and over again, this moon will bring sudden clarity – a new way of seeing not only situations and other people, but also you. It will help you to see what you did not see before and realise how you can do things differently.

The sun is in Sagittarius during this full moon, so the themes of Sagittarius – such as being a free spirit, independence and an eternal quest for knowledge – will now be highlighted by this full moon with Gemini energy added to them.

Use the combined energy of these two lively, inquisitive signs to really begin to find clarity, answers and knowledge, including self-knowledge. If you have found yourself stuck so far this year, this full moon will help you to begin to see a way forward and new ways of doing things, as neither of these signs likes to dwell in the past.

Use the Gemini full moon to . . .

✳ . . . notice the inner narrative in your head. Take note of any repetitive questions or criticisms and release these under the waning moon.

✳ . . . notice the same patterns and situations you constantly find yourself in. Make a list of them, try to see what they have shown/taught you up to now and how you can do things differently going forward.

✳ . . . look forward, not back. Notice where you tend to stay stuck in the past and, for each past experience you find yourself reliving, write down one way you can alter that to move forward instead.

The keywords for Gemini are 'I THINK'

Use this as a journal prompt and see what flows to you in answer. Set some intentions or create some affirmations (see p. 187) using this declaration at the beginning – things like:

- ✤ I THINK kind and loving thoughts.
- ✤ I THINK that change is wonderful.
- ✤ I THINK that all my dreams are coming true.

What to watch out for under a Gemini moon:

1 Speaking too much and using a hundred words when you could use two.

2 Which twin you are feeding – you have a choice in each moment.

3 Getting easily bored, restless or impatient; your attention span will be zero!

 A crystal for this moon: danburite for change and leaving the past behind, blue calcite to bring clarity to the confusion and quieten the mind chatter or blue lace agate for communication

CHAPTER 8:

The Moon in Cancer

The moon to be in ebb and flow

Element: *Water*
Quality: *Cardinal*
Ruling planet: *The Moon*
Symbol: *The Crab*

THE CANCER MOON teaches us all about ebb and flow, as it uncovers emotions, insights, vulnerabilities and our deepest intuition.

MY MOON MUSINGS

Cancer is the watery sign of emotions, so don't be surprised if you feel overly sensitive for a few days around this moon. The moon rules Cancer, and so just as she affects the tides, you may experience this same ebb and flow in your emotions, going from the highest of highs to the lowest of lows.

These emotions are surfacing for a reason though, and there is no way to hide under a Cancer moon. Anything and everything you have suppressed, are unwilling to see or hear or address or have been avoiding will come bubbling back up to the surface for you to deal with, learn from and, once and for all, release. Rather than get caught up in this emotional turmoil, the moon in Cancer gives you a real opportunity to create change. This is an important moon for reflecting on the stories you have created for yourself, the emotions you allow to be triggered by certain people and situations, the illusions you've formed about your life, where you're feeling stuck and your deepest, darkest insecurities.

Spend some time with these inner reflections and your emotions. Journal on what you are feeling and see if you can get to the root cause of where these emotions come from. You may find that the feeling you get when your boss ignores you comes from a deeply ingrained feeling of not being good enough. Or when your partner doesn't understand your point of view it compounds a lifelong story you tell yourself that you are never heard or listened to. Cancer doesn't like small talk and so cuts through to the emotional centre, right to the heart of the matter. And it's from discovering these truths and their root causes that lasting healing can take place.

It's one thing to declare change and what you want, it's another to act on it. As humans, we don't like too much change and the Cancerian crab tends to avoid any conflict, scuttling sideways to get away, rather than facing anything head on. As such, this moon will highlight all the ways in which you declare freedom for yourself and set intentions, only to then pull your crab-like shell around yourself to prevent failure or getting hurt, or scuttle away in denial to avoid confrontation. The Cancer moon will help you to see and face up to all of this and move forward, despite the doubts and emotions.

Cancer represents the feminine, the mother energy and is associated with home, family and feeling safe and grounded. This moon calls you into taking care of your inner home – your heart and soul – and ensuring that you don't put the needs of others way above your own.

You may find you are called into your shell to tend to your own needs during this moon. Please listen to this and act on it. This moon is one that gives you the courage and power to gently set boundaries and make necessary changes so that you can begin to put your own needs first and focus more on self-love and self-care. Remember that you can't pour from an empty cup. Cancer teaches you that, just like our beautiful moon, you also need ebb and flow, times of brightness and being out there, and times of introspection and rest. If you can learn to flow in this way, you will notice huge shifts in your ability to take care of yourself and those around you.

Cancer has a motherly energy and wants you to feel safe and protected, nurtured and loved, and you may find this moon calling you into taking back your power in any areas of your life where you don't feel this way. This moon will help you set boundaries with people who take too much, to say no to situations that don't make you feel comfortable, to walk away from uncertain or unloving relationships and to take care and protect yourself the way a mother would a child.

This moon also brings vulnerability to the forefront. As important as it is to retreat into your shell for self-care, you may find that you use it for protection against life; but this moon asks you to break down the shell you have built to protect yourself from fear, failure, intimacy and love. Cancer is a moon that helps you to lean into and face your vulnerabilities in order to achieve your goals.

THE CANCER MOON CALLS YOU INTO . . .

. . . shedding your shell and being vulnerable. Allow this moon to show you what you keep under lock and key. Listen to your heart and soul and be completely honest with yourself. Speaking up is so important under this moon, so open your heart and share with those close to you your needs, your desires, your fears and, most of all, your vulnerabilities. Your intuition, insight and inner guidance will be at their absolute peak under this moon, so listen to, trust and believe them. They will never be wrong.

THE MOON RULES CANCER

Taking us deeper into the ebb and flow of our emotions and inner selves. The moon is truly at home in Cancer, and so this is one of the best moons for connecting with Lunar Living and the gifts that getting in touch with your inner world holds. This moon is connected to the heart chakra and will help to show you how to fulfil your emotional needs, and any ways that you have built a shell around your heart or developed unhealthy emotional attachments.

NEW MOON IN CANCER – FALLS IN CANCER SEASON BETWEEN 21 JUNE AND 22 JULY

Cancer season marks the beginning of summer and brings us the summer solstice.

Nature has opened the door to the second half of the year, so use this moon to help you plan for it and to open that new chapter in your life.

As Cancer is the sign of intuition, self-care, feminine power and deep nurturing, this new moon, more than ever, is a time to put yourself first, especially if you spend all your time putting everyone else's needs before your own. Set aside some quality time under this moon to take care of yourself – perhaps take a day off work to do something you've been meaning to do for months or block out a weekend to spend time at a spa or with old friends.

This is a moon for embracing and accepting your emotions and using them as signposts, being emotionally available and truly present with others and letting down your crab-like shell to see your vulnerability as a strength.

Use the Cancer new moon to . . .

✸ **. . . review your spring equinox intentions (the ones you set at the start of the astrological new year at the Aries new moon).** Look at what came true, what didn't and why. Make any necessary changes to your intentions for this next three-month cycle.

✸ **. . . come back home to yourself.** Nurture, nourish and be very gentle with yourself under this moon. Dedicate an hour or more a day over the new moon to something that makes you feel at home. This is also a wonderful moon for snuggling up in your home and feeling it take care of you, also taking the opportunity to tell all your family and friends what they mean to you.

✸ **. . . uncover your emotions.** Get inside your shell, through all the human insecurities and doubts and right into the depths of your truth, your wisdom and the voice of your soul. Journaling can be a great tool for this (see p. 191) and you can then use these deep insights to see how to move forward through the waxing phase.

FULL MOON IN CANCER – FALLS IN CAPRICORN SEASON BETWEEN 22 DECEMBER AND 19 JANUARY

This is the first full moon following the winter solstice, and as we enter back into the light, it feels like darkness has been lifted, as though under the light of this full moon you can finally see the truth.

Under this guiding full moon light, your path ahead will become clear, so use the deep intensity of this full moon to let go of anything standing in the way of what you want to create and achieve for the beginning of the traditional new year.

If you tune in and truly 'feel' into your gut feelings, your intuition, your wisdom, your heart, the very depths of your being, everything you need to know will become clear under the heartfelt intuitive guidance of this dreamy full moon.

The sun is in Capricorn during this full moon, so the themes of Capricorn – such as shaking foundations, long-term visions and ambition – will now be highlighted by this full moon with Cancer energy added to them.

The practical nature of Capricorn will help you make sense of the depths of the emotions stirred by the cancer moon, give you clarity about where you are stuck and show you where, how and to whom you give your power away. If you find yourself second-guessing and doubting the path ahead, incorporate some mountain-goat Capricorn energy to plan and strategise the way forward.

Use the Cancer full moon to . . .

✹ . . . make a clear plan of what needs to change. List all the changes that you would like to make in your life and make a plan of how you can do this, even if it's long-term. Use the waning moon to start to let things go.

✹ **. . . cleanse your home.** As the Cancer moon is strongly associated with the home, use this moon to release from it anything you no longer need. It's a good time to use a smudge or sage stick to cleanse the energies in your home and to have a clear-out of anything that you have been hoarding.

✹ **. . . shed your shell.** Use this moon to shine a light on where you have built up a hard shell of protection around yourself for fear of being judged, failing or not wanting to appear weak or vulnerable. Use the waning moon to allow these structures and parts of you to gently fall away.

The keywords for Cancer are 'I FEEL'

Use this as a journal prompt and see what flows to you in answer. Set some intentions or create some affirmations (see p. 187), using this declaration at the beginning – things like:

✹ I FEEL at home in myself.
✹ I FEEL nurtured and protected.
✹ I FEEL safe to be vulnerable.

What to watch out for under a Cancer moon:

1 Becoming moody and emotionally unpredictable.

2 Avoidance of facing up to things and clinging too
   tightly to what you know must go.

3 Withdrawing into and hiding in your shell.

 A crystal for this moon: pink fluorite for your
emotions, carnelian for confidence in moving forward
through fear or moonstone to work more deeply with
the moon's wisdom

CHAPTER 9:

The Moon in Leo

The moon to feel liberated

Element: *Fire*
Quality: *Fixed*
Ruling planet: *The Sun*
Symbol: *The Lion*

A LEO MOON often brings with it a little glimmer of light and hope, a feeling of relief and possibly even a new-found confidence.

MY MOON MUSINGS

Leo's ruling planet is the sun and Leo is the fiery sign that rules the heart, meaning this moon helps you to realise the unique gifts to the universe that radiate from your heart only. Leo wants you to be completely and utterly your most authentic self – to feel liberated and fearlessly share your one-off self out into the world.

Playful Leo helps to override all those 'adult responsibilities', which often make your dreams and desires feel like pipe dreams. Instead, Leo is like an excitable child, joyful and inspired by just about anything and everything. Leo tells us that life is an adventure and, most of all, that it should be fun.

So often 'adulting' puts our biggest desires and passions on the back burner. Life, responsibilities, to-do lists, ifs, buts and maybes all get in the way and life can become monotonous. Leo wants to know what you would do in this moment if 'real life' wasn't in the way. Beneath all the layers and labels, who are you really, and what do you desire, deep down in your heart? Leo wants you to find freedom in self-expression and creativity, to liberate yourself from any captivity in your life and to release your inner king of the jungle, so as to rule your heart and inner domain from a place of love and freedom.

Of course we have a certain level of responsibility in life, but the moon in Leo calls for you to put yourself first a bit more, to notice how you possibly sacrifice yourself by putting the needs, happiness and goals of others before your own.

This moon is here to ignite your heart, boost your self-belief, lift your spirits and let your soul soar. With Leo energy, you will find the power to break free of the internal beliefs and bonds that block your dreams.

One thing that Leo does demand though is that you take complete responsibility for your own life, your actions and everything that has brought you to this moment. A Leo moon reminds you of your power. In each moment, you have a choice, and whether you make those choices consciously or not, *you* are always choosing the way your life is heading. You need to stop blaming misfortunes on others. Taking back the power and responsibility puts you in control and gives you back leadership of your life. This moon is a call to action. As you begin to show up more for yourself, life will start to show up more for you.

As the ruler of the heart, Leo wants you to be able to live fully and completely in and from your heart. But in order to access it you have to remove all that keeps it closed, protected and shut. When you close off your heart, you close off your wisdom and ability to feel and to know – that deep inner knowing which can guide your life if you choose to follow its whispers. In order to help you to access the full capacity of your beautiful, wise, loving heart, this moon often brings up all that remains raw and unresolved, so that you can become aware of it to heal it.

As this healing happens, you may find that under this moon you get perfect clarity in your heart that you have outgrown people, situations, jobs and beliefs. As the king of the jungle starts to stir within you, opening your heart, you will begin to truly step into your power and realise and release anything that does not align with your grand future Leo vision for yourself.

THE LEO MOON CALLS YOU INTO . . .

. . . thinking big, acting bold and living from your heart. The Leo moon energy allows you that deep delve into your heart to get to know, love and trust yourself on a very deep, intuitive level. The truth of your entire being – all that's come before, all that's possible and yet to come, and all that you

are capable of – will be shown to you if you allow the courageous lion to lead you deep into your heart.

THE SUN RULES LEO

The sun is the giver of life and light and power. You only
have to look around at how much more happy, energised
and alive everyone is when the sun shines to know that.
The sun is associated with the solar-plexus chakra (see
p. 30), your own personal inner sunshine. This bright
yellow glowing ball of inner sunshine is your centre of
power, energy, will and achievement. This is the place from
which you manifest and magnetise towards you all that
you want to create in the world. Use the energy of Leo
and the sun to make yourself magnetic to all that you
desire and to shine your light out into the world.

NEW MOON IN LEO – FALLS IN LEO SEASON
BETWEEN 23 JULY AND 22 AUGUST

This is a wonderful moon under which to get clear on how
you wish to speak your truth and share your heartfelt gift
and authentic voice with the world. You may tell me that
you don't have one, but believe me you do, and Leo will help
you find and feel it.

You will find a deep desire under this moon to do work
that is of service to the world and humanity and to share

something that only you can share, and so if you've had any ideas about starting something new, Leo is your perfect partner for heart-based endeavours or plans to bring you and the world joy, even if you're not sure exactly how yet. This moon will give you the bravery to take on new things and the commitment to see them through.

This is also a wonderful moon for self-care, as Leo energy makes giving yourself permission for rest and pampering a lot easier, so put your needs first for a day or two. Give yourself some down time so you have the energy for all the play that's to come. Just as you often see lionesses lying around all day, basking in the sun, so that they'll have the energy to go after what they want later in the day, you should allow yourself the same luxurious stretching out and gathering back of your energy.

Use the Leo new moon to . . .

✸ **. . . listen to your heart's calling.** Place your hands over your heart for just a few moments every day to tune in to how it feels and to receive any messages it's trying to send you.

✸ **. . . find your inner spark of self-expression.** For ten minutes a day, do something that lights you up; it could be writing, painting, dancing, singing – whatever you feel most expresses the inner you in that moment.

✸ **. . . have more fun, play and adventure.** Plan two or three activities over the waxing moon to bring more happiness, joy and childlike energy into your life.

FULL MOON IN LEO – FALLS IN AQUARIUS SEASON
BETWEEN 20 JANUARY AND 18 FEBRUARY

A Leo full moon always brings a roar! Leo brings with it the fire to move things along, to burn through all that's standing in the way and to awaken your passions and desires. Leo helps you to stand up and be seen and heard, to take back the power and control of your own life and to be in touch with your own needs – and whatever makes you roar.

Under a Leo full moon, let the lion show you that anything is possible. It's time to reconnect back into your heart, your truth and your courage, strength and inner wisdom. Stop listening to fear and start listening to your heart, loving more than you fear and being brave and bold. It's time to shine, to be unapologetically, authentically you and to let go of anything that stands in the way of that.

The sun is in Aquarius during this full moon, so the themes of Aquarius – such as freedom-seeking, rebellion and human-itarian action – will now be highlighted by this full moon with Leo energy added to them.

If you're feeling trapped, find freedom and liberation in the simplest of things. Take an hour out while the kids are at school to visit somewhere you haven't been before or head out of the office on your lunch break, rather than being tied to the desk. If you feel a call to create, carve out just ten minutes a day to be in your creative expression: sing, dance, paint – do whatever makes your heart come to life. Find ways that you can use your big, beautiful heart to be of service, even if that's just being there for a friend or colleague in need.

Use the Leo full moon to . . .

✳ . . . burn through all that is standing in the way of your passion and desires. Use the fiery Leo energy to make a list of all the doubts and fears that you allow to hold you back.

✳ . . . get clear on where you sacrifice your dreams for reality. Make a list of all of the dreams you had before life got in the way, or things you would do right now if there were no responsibilities. Find little ways to include these things in your life through the waning moon.

✳ . . . forgive. Leo shows you how to keep your heart open, even through hardships, so use this moon to write a list of all the people you need to forgive, including yourself. Use the waning-moon cycle to keep releasing any hurts you hold in your heart.

The keywords for Leo are 'I WILL'

Use this as a journal prompt and see what flows to you in answer. Set some intentions or create some affirmations using this declaration at the beginning – things like:

✳ I WILL open my heart and forgive.
✳ I WILL have more fun, excitement and adventure.
✳ I WILL be brave and bold and roar.

What to watch out for under a Leo moon:

1 Telling people what you think they want to hear, rather than speaking the truth.

2 Being a drama queen or throwing childlike tantrums.

3 Giving unsolicited advice to everyone around you, even though it comes from a good place.

 A crystal for this moon: rose quartz for opening your heart, sunstone for self-empowerment and to harness the energy of the sun or amazonite to bring childlike playfulness

CHAPTER 10

The Moon in Virgo

The moon to make an action plan

Element: *Earth*
Quality: *Mutable*
Ruling planet: *Mercury, the planet of communication*
Symbol: *The Virgin*

SOLID AND EARTHY, the Virgo moon comes along to help you move forward towards very real, very grounded dreams from a very real, very grounded place.

MY MOON MUSINGS

The most practical of moons, Virgo asks you to look at the here and now, as it's only from this present moment that you can make change. Rather than wallowing in or being held back by a long-gone past or living in some imagined future moment where you'll do it all when everything is 'perfect', this moon wants you to instead get real, right here, right now. To do this, Virgo will literally bring you back down to earth, back to life, back to reality.

This could be a bumpy landing for some of you, especially if you tend to lean towards escapism, avoidance or making yourself so busy your feet don't touch the ground. It's in this present-moment reality check that this moon holds the most intensity and the most healing, more so if you are confronted with the truth that here is not where you want or planned to be.

Virgo, with its critical, perfectionist, demanding energy, will show you clearly how you have never felt good enough, or worthy enough. This moon will bring that voice and your deepest inner critic rushing to the surface – because they are what truly holds you back from taking action towards every one of your dreams and from being truly yourself in relationships and friendships, saying yes to great opportunities and fully embracing life.

This can make Virgo a deeply emotional moon, as you realise how you have always sabotaged what you want in life by criticising (yourself or others) or that you are always waiting for things to be perfect before going after what you want, or that you didn't believe you deserved what you want.

This is where the deep healing of this moon comes in – because now that you know the voice of the inner critic and these deep-rooted beliefs exist, you can work on healing them. Virgo in its present-moment awareness helps you to see that you are not your thoughts and beliefs, and that you can work on healing and changing them at any time.

The sign of the healer and virgin goddess Virgo guides you into deep inner healing – into creating a whole new set of thoughts and beliefs and reality for yourself. You are one thought or belief away from changing your entire life.

Virgo also helps you to find your deep intuition and knowing – the part of you that trusts and believes. Virgo aligns you back with nature, so if you've been struggling to find a deep connection with the moon or cycles or transitions and change, this moon will help you with that. Virgo is deeply connected to the earth, trusting in the wisdom and abundance of nature and that everything is happening in perfect order. Virgo loves sorting and synchronicity and lining everything up so that the universe, or 'higher power' or Source, or nature – or whatever word you call it – can assist in getting things done.

Now, with all this new-found knowledge and healing, it's time to put real change and action into place. From knowing where you are right now you can make a clear action plan to get to where you want to be. This moon will give you a much-needed boost of inspiration and the drive to get things done. If you have felt resistance to change, Virgo brings fresh, new inspiration and a plan to make this a moon of real, grounded new beginnings.

THE VIRGO MOON CALLS YOU INTO . . .

. . . taking action. This moon will help you get things off the ground, push along new projects and make any changes that need to be made, problem solve, multitask, meet demands, get organised and take on new and exciting challenges. Virgo will help you to know exactly how you will get there. Efficient, detail-driven, hard-working Virgo will help you to plan, and plan and plan some more – to tweak and drill down into details until you get it just right. Virgo will bring you all the tools, insight, knowledge, enthusiasm and drive to make your dream a reality.

MERCURY, THE PLANET OF COMMUNICATION, RULES VIRGO

Under the Virgo moon it can be a wonderful time to notice your communication style. How do you speak to yourself on a daily basis? Is your inner narrative one of perfectionism and criticism? Can you turn that around with some positive affirmations (see p. 187)? With those around you, are you always jumping in with your perfectionist practical advice or seeing what needs fixing and criticising (even if it's well intended)? How can you communicate with yourself and others in a more kind and effective way?

NEW MOON IN VIRGO – FALLS IN VIRGO SEASON BETWEEN 23 AUGUST AND 22 SEPTEMBER

This moon can bring a 'back-to-school' feeling with it and you may feel like there is so much to do but you don't quite know what or how.

Under this new moon you may find the voice of 'not enough' and your deepest inner critic rushing to the surface. You may find yourself trying to do things but because they're not 'perfect', you keep swapping and changing and comparing and criticising.

You may be called to real alone time under this new moon. Allow that. Use whatever comes up for you under this new moon as an opportunity to put yourself first, taking care of your inner and outer wellbeing and creating space for yourself and your healing.

The trick under this new moon is not to allow the emotion to take over, but to use the Virgo energy to organise, plan, create and focus your attention on where you want to be. Your emotions about your present-moment reality are your signposts for what needs to change.

Use the Virgo new moon to . . .

❋ ... **be present.** Use this time to stop, listen, get grounded, present and real. Where are you in your life right now? What would need to change in this moment to take you towards more happiness, more wholeness and more purpose? Take note of the discoveries you make in this time of slowing down and remember that it is only from being in this present moment and making real present-moment changes that you can create a lasting difference.

❋ ... **make a plan.** Be methodical and put daily, weekly and monthly goals in place; Virgo loves

routine and structure, which can create a hugely
supportive foundation for any new beginnings
that need to happen to lead you towards
happiness.

✦ . . . go 'back to school'. Virgo has a huge passion for
learning, so this moon will help you to gain
knowledge and wisdom, clarity and belief in any
areas of your life in which you have previously felt
uncertain or doubted yourself. What can you learn or
study over the waxing moon?

FULL MOON IN VIRGO – FALLS IN PISCES SEASON BETWEEN 19 FEBRUARY AND 20 MARCH

Virgo is an extremely grounded earth sign, meaning that you
can't hide, fantasise, pretend or make excuses under this
moon. This moon is almost like a celestial slap that brings
you back to reality and means that everything will suddenly
become obvious to you: where you are, what you are doing,
what you are allowing yourself to put up with, the gut feelings you are hearing/ignoring, the way your fears control
you, what is weighing you down, where you are stuck and,
most of all, what needs to change in order for you to be
happy.

This moon will ground you firmly in reality – your reality
–asking you to look it right in the eye. Do you like what you
see? Is this how you pictured your life? For some of you,
the answer is going to be a big yes, and everything will feel

exciting as you get to put even bigger plans in place. For others, it will be an emotional ride as you wonder how you got here and need to delve into the reality of your situation and what changes need to be made.

The sun is in Pisces during this full moon, so the themes of Pisces – such as imagination, sensitive emotion and closing chapters – will now be highlighted by this full moon with Virgo energy added to them.

Allow dreamy imaginative Pisces to infuse your Virgo practical present-moment reality. These two signs are a wonderful combination under a full moon, as Pisces helps you to create endings, gives you the ability to dream and vision your future, while Virgo puts the practical plans in place to make it happen.

Use the Virgo full moon to . . .

✴ **. . . put your life under scrutiny (in a kind and gentle way, of course).** Used in the right way, Virgo energy can be quite transformative. Practical, organised Virgo will help you to examine everything, so you can sort through your life, find order and make firm plans towards your future.

✴ **. . . let go of the inner critic and doubt.** If the Virgo moon has your self-critic, doubter and overthinking mind going into overdrive, take time to notice what the narrative is. Write down the most common stories and work on releasing them under the waning moon.

✱ . . . **get practical about what you can change**. Virgo has no time for self-pity and wallowing and instead wants practical logic and grounded present-moment change. Try asking, 'What could I do right now to change this situation?' and put plans in motion under the waning moon.

The keywords for Virgo are 'I ANALYSE'

Use this as a journal prompt and see what flows to you in answer. Set some intentions or create some affirmations (see p. 187), using this declaration at the beginning – things like:

✱ I ANALYSE my present-moment reality.
✱ I ANALYSE the voice of my inner critic and doubt.
✱ I ANALYSE my way forward, creating a clear action plan.

What to watch out for under a Virgo moon:

1 The perfectionist that will only allow you to move forward when it's 'perfect' (your life is a work in progress and will never be 'perfect').

2 The criticism, the nagging, the demands, the not enough . . .

3 Over-planning and organising to the point where you
don't leave any room for universal guidance or something even better to come along.

 A crystal for this moon: fluorite for creating an
action plan, peridot to connect you to nature and help
release negative thought patterns or howlite to help
with the inner critic

CHAPTER 11:

The Moon in Libra

The moon to find balance and heal relationships

Element: *Air*
Quality: *Cardinal*
Ruling planet: *Venus, the planet of love*
Symbol: *The Scales*

LIKE SCALES, YOU may tip from one extreme to the other, as this moon helps you to find balance in all areas of your life.

MY MOON MUSINGS

Balance, balance, balance is what this moon is calling you to. However, this moon can feel wobbly, unbalanced and indecisive – there will be push, pull, yes, no, I'm ready, I'm not . . .

Indecision can be a trait of a Libra moon, especially when it comes to facing or dealing with obvious problems in your life. It may feel easier to sit on the fence or hide until it all goes away, but you can't, and it won't.

Instead, you may find this moon reveals truths, cracks open the walls you erect around your heart, brings about forced change in your situation, pushes you to have those conversations you have been putting off, breaks things open, pulls them down, shakes them up – you get the idea! All in the name of bringing balance back into your life, of course.

If you have been struggling to keep on top of things or commit to decisions, procrastinating over moving forward, doing too much and burning out, not setting or sticking to clear boundaries, allowing something or someone to take up too much of your time and energy or hiding from the truth, this moon is here to bring you back to balance.

The Libra moon brings a particular focus to your relationships – with the people around you, with yourself and with life. You will find that you question romantic relationships and whether or not they are working, if they feel unstable or out of balance in any areas. If you give more than you receive, that will become obvious, in a romantic sense and also in friendships. Family dynamics and expectations can also come to the forefront under this moon. It's like a big mirror reflecting your life back to you – and you could finally get to see what you have been avoiding seeing for a long time.

This means that emotional insecurity can be huge under this moon, along with feelings of inadequacy. The wisdom of this moon is in helping you to truly understand that relief from these feelings must come from within. No relationship can ever give you what you don't already believe in your heart about yourself. Notice what you seek out in the relationships in your life (approval, love, security, etc.) and begin to find ways to cultivate more of that for yourself. You need to become your own best friend under this moon.

This moon also helps you to see any unhealed issues that continue to play out in your personal interactions. It helps you to understand the motivations behind your actions and whether you act from a place of fear, love, a need for approval, etc. Most of all, this moon helps you to see how your inner world creates your outer, and that it is only through deep healing, self-love, compassion, truth, boundaries, self-care and self-belief that true balance in life can occur: you have to receive as much as you give and give as much as you receive.

Which brings us to the most important relationship of all, the one you have with yourself. Do you fully believe in and support yourself, as you would expect a best friend to? Do you love and honour and adore yourself in the way you hope a lover would? Do you speak kindly and positively to yourself? What is your story with yourself? You have to become your own cheerleader, supporter and best friend – and this moon highlights that. The Libra moon helps you to open up to and listen to the intelligence and wisdom of your heart. Libra is a sign that loves love, to love and be loved – and that love has to start at home.

Loving and respecting yourself enough to put you and your wants and needs first is key under this moon; it will enable you to make informed decisions and set intentions that align with your heart and soul. That's not to say that you don't need to consider others, but if your decisions are *always* based on other people and their needs and/or out of fear, that will become obvious under this moon, as the compass of your heart shows you how you are giving your one precious life away. Your love for you needs to become greater than your desire to please others.

This moon helps you to find balance between doing and being, pushing and surrendering, pulling and releasing, giving and receiving, chasing your dreams and trusting in the perfection of the universe and allowing it to all unfold just as it should. Allow the scales to tip to find balance.

THE LIBRA MOON CALLS YOU INTO . . .

. . . remaining true to you, not giving away too much to your own detriment and practising self-care. Libra will show you clearly where you are living life by other people's needs and desires and doing things that aren't aligned with your values. This will be extremely obvious and uncomfortable under this moon. The magic of this moon is in allowing the scales to tip, to gently and lovingly release from your life all that keeps you out of balance and to invite in more of what you really want.

VENUS, THE PLANET OF LOVE, RULES LIBRA

Your ability to love and be loved, and all your relationships, will be highlighted under this moon. Libra likes us to keep things balanced, and so this moon, in particular, will bring up unresolved, unhealed and unspoken relationship concerns, so that you can process them. Loneliness can also be an issue under this moon, especially if you avoid relationships or true intimacy due to past hurts. Allow yourself to feel your feelings, relive any memories and even to cry a little if you need to; tears under this moon are like a rain shower – they will come, cleanse everything away and go, leaving it all a little bit brighter and more balanced than before.

NEW MOON IN LIBRA – FALLS IN LIBRA SEASON BETWEEN 23 SEPTEMBER AND 22 OCTOBER

Libra season brings the autumn equinox, and the Libra new moon comes along to begin a new season. While every new moon brings the chance of a new beginning, change is definitely in the autumn air with this one.

Use the Libra new moon to really go inwards and listen. Just as nature and the nights are drawing in all around you, this time of deep introspection is key to beginning the new season in a clear and focused way. This drawing in is a beautiful opportunity to nurture the inner world of your hopes and dreams and get back on track with anything that got lost along the way in the height of summer.

Under this new moon it's time to set your intentions for the autumn season and to put in motion anything that you want to make true for you before the winter solstice, and the closing of the traditional year.

Use the Libra new moon to . . .

✳ **. . . get clear on your autumn intentions.** Make a list of three to five things you will achieve over the next three months through the autumn season and before the traditional year closes.

✳ **. . . practise self-care and self-love.** Specifically, practise the inner self-care of listening to your heart and soul. Dedicate a time every day over the waxing-moon cycle to take care of yourself.

✳ **. . . create healthier bonds and boundaries.** With relationships under the moonlight, this is a good moon under which to look at your bonds and boundaries in relationships. Do you give enough gratitude to the people who fill your life with joy and are always there to support you? And how strong are your boundaries when it comes to the takers in your life? How much do you give, give, give with nothing in return?

FULL MOON IN LIBRA – FALLS IN ARIES SEASON BETWEEN 21 MARCH AND 19 APRIL

Full moons can amplify emotions at the best of times, but you may find feelings of insecurity, comparison and indecision run high under this airy full moon. You may find it difficult to make sense of your emotions, to believe in yourself and even the simplest decisions could feel like hard work.

It might seem as though everyone else is blossoming and you are tightly wound up in bud with no idea how to get out! It's under this moon that you could most feel you are being 'left behind' in life, and the frantic energy of the moon may make you want to run out there and do something – anything.

The sun is in Aries during this full moon, so the themes of Aries – such as enthusiasm, courage and new beginnings – will now be highlighted by this full moon with Libra energy added to them.

Aries is the first sign of the zodiac and begins the astrological year, and so although all full moons are a time of completion, this one really needs you to ensure that you release all that weighs you down and keeps your life out of balance, so that the new season and astrological year can be different.

See your life as a set of scales and this moon as a huge opportunity to help you to find balance. What do you need to take off your scales to lighten your emotional load? What do you need to add so that you come into your full blossom and potential?

Use the Libra full moon to . . .

✸ . . . take stock of the relationships in your life (including the one you have with yourself). Notice where things are out of balance in the give-and-take stakes and either take action to bring them more into a state of balance or consider whether any relationships could have run their course.

✴ **. . . speak your truth**. The waning moon is the perfect time to share your feelings and perhaps lean into the vulnerability that keeps you from being authentic and showing up in relationships. Libra has a tendency to avoid confrontation and difficult conversations, but these are needed in order to find true balance and harmony in relationships. So if you have left things unsaid for too long, now may be the time to restore balance and say them.

✴ **. . . do the inner healing of relationship wounds, triggers or outdated beliefs.** Notice which old relationships, hurts or stories keep coming back up and take some time to process and 'complete' these. What did the relationship teach you, and how can you learn from this and move on?

The keywords for Libra are 'I BALANCE'

Use this as a journal prompt and see what flows to you in answer. Set some intentions or create some affirmations (see p.187), using this declaration at the beginning – things like:

✴ I BALANCE giving with receiving.
✴ I BALANCE my needs with the needs of all of those around me.
✴ I BALANCE my heart and my soul.

What to watch out for under a Libra moon:

1 Emotional insecurity and inadequacy and putting the blame for them on other people and situations.

2 Making excuses for other people and their behaviours to avoid confrontation or letting go.

3 So much indecisiveness and uncertainty that you become frozen and instead do nothing.

 A crystal for this moon: magnesite for calming the emotions and self-love, tiger's eye for balance or chrysocolla for relationship healing

CHAPTER 12:

The Moon in Scorpio

The moon to change and transform

Element: *Water*
Quality: *Fixed*
Ruling planet: *Pluto, the lord of the underworld and planet of transformation*
Symbol: *The Scorpion*

THIS IS A moon for the brave – for those who desire to know more, have more and aren't afraid to do both the internal and external work it takes to get there.

MY MOON MUSINGS

A moon in Scorpio is a no-holds-barred game changer. It's intense and emotion-filled; it's a deep dive beneath the surface and if you are willing to go there, its powerful energy brings a huge opportunity for change and transformation.

This moon is here to cut through all the illusions and half-truths you tell yourself daily about how everything is ok, and instead pull back the curtain for a big reveal of what is really going on underneath. The Scorpio moon helps you to take off all the masks you wear as you try to be all things to everybody and put on a brave face for the outside world. As deep truths are uncovered and everything you have been hiding comes bubbling up to the surface, emotions may be deep and all-consuming.

Scorpio is the sign of death and rebirth, and so change is coming under this moon whether you like it or not. It's up to you whether you are the instigator of that change or a so-called victim of circumstance. This is your baptism of fire for deep growth and self-acceptance, allowing parts of you to die so that you can be reborn. This is an opportunity to get to know you like never before.

You may find, just to test this further, that catalysts and triggers for your deep, hidden emotions and limiting self-beliefs will come up over this moon. Don't suppress anything. Take responsibility for your emotions and how you have ended up where you are. This is important as it helps you to become an active participant in your own transformation and rebirth. Embrace your emotions and allow them to show you the way.

Scorpio loves a mystery and won't stop until it finds the truth, and so the trick to this moon is to take that deep dive beneath the surface, into the murky waters and the parts you hide from – the little shadow selves and feelings of inadequacy that stay hidden just around the corner, waiting to jump out on you at any given moment; the secret fears, the not enough, the imposter, the shame.

This is one of the best moons to do emotional healing

and shadow work (see p. 29), as you just can't hide from your deep inner truths, desires and demons under a Scorpio moon. Use what is coming up for you to uncover subtle truths about areas in your life in which you need to make change, no matter how uncomfortable or confusing these truths may seem.

It's time to be honest with yourself, as it's only through facing your fears, anxieties, the 'not good enough voice' and the parts of your life that you try to run from that you can fully own and release these things.

This moon is here to reveal your soul plan and your purpose, but you will have to dive deep to find it.

THE SCORPIO MOON CALLS YOU INTO . . .

. . . feeling all the feelings. Scorpio is one of the most emotional and intuitive signs and so brings with it an opportunity for deep transformation, healing and power. Use this moon to tap into your emotions to get in touch with not only what you truly want, but also what has been standing in your way: what are your self-destruct patterns? How do you keep yourself small? In which ways do you self-doubt and always play it safe? Give yourself time to slow down, honour, explore and process your emotions. Let this moon guide you into your inner world – the one you bury beneath the surface. You won't find the answers you are seeking externally; they are hidden within the murky depths, waiting for you to find them. This is a hugely powerful, potential-filled, life-changing moon, but only for those brave enough to take the road less travelled, to delve deep, face the fears, do the work, hold up the mirror and, most of all, to embrace the dark to get to the light.

PLUTO, LORD OF THE UNDERWORLD AND PLANET OF TRANSFORMATION, RULES SCORPIO

Pluto is the planet of death and rebirth, destruction and illuminating the shadows of our consciousness. But rather than something to be feared, Pluto helps us to overcome any blocks, clearing the way for something new. Pluto brings the things we hide in the dark into the light, so that they can be healed and transformed. Before Pluto was discovered in 1930, Mars (the planet of war) ruled Scorpio, meaning that under this moon you will face your transformation like a warrior, fighting for what you want and stepping into your power.

NEW MOON IN SCORPIO – FALLS IN SCORPIO SEASON BETWEEN 23 OCTOBER AND 21 NOVEMBER

Intense is one of the best ways to describe this new moon, as it asks you to dive deep into your emotions, into the shadows, the hidden and the unknown.

As you delve into yourself, especially the parts you hide from others, use this new-moon time to acknowledge, accept and heal these parts of yourself with compassion, self-love and kindness.

This moon will help you to see the truth behind your actions, take down barriers that you have built and access deep levels of healing. It's a moon of great vulnerability, but if you can lean into this, sharing from your heart, facing your fears, letting go of the need to be strong or right or in control – this moon will take you to new levels of potential and real transformation.

Use the Scorpio new moon to . . .

🌟 . . . **ask yourself those deep soul questions.** Am I speaking and living my truth? Am I happy? Am I carrying old emotions and resentments? Am I stuck in the same cycles repeating the same things over and over? Am I celebrating my achievements or playing small?

🌟 . . . **use your emotions as signposts**. Use the emotional intensity of this moon to make sense of where you want to go in your life. Make a list of your deep emotions, and in which life areas you experience them over this moon. Under each one, journal what this emotion may be signposting you to. Use the waxing moon to take action in these areas.

🌟 . . . **get clear on your barriers, boundaries, avoidance tactics and protection systems.** Notice what you do to avoid being vulnerable or feeling too much. Decide on ways you can allow yourself to be more vulnerable through the waxing moon.

FULL MOON IN SCORPIO – FALLS IN TAURUS
SEASON BETWEEN 20 APRIL AND 20 MAY

This is a full moon that packs its punches and shines the brightest full-moon light on all your shadows. Under this full moon it's likely that you will feel as though anything and everything you have ever tried to suppress or hide from is resurfacing. You'll feel exhausted, yet in the wide-awake club, identifying so clearly with that well-known meme: 'My mind is like an Internet browser – 20 tabs open, 3 are frozen and I have no idea where the music is coming from.'

The sun is in Taurus during this full moon, so the themes of Taurus – such as nurturing, self-care, safety and security – will now be highlighted by this full moon with Scorpio energy added to them.

The combination of these two signs can be powerful and healing as Taurus – the nurturing energy that calls you back home to yourself and asks you to slow down and tune in – allows you the time and a safe space under this intense full moon to do the inner emotional processing. This is a moon to accept and love all the parts of yourself, even those you try to hide from the world or deny, are ashamed of or want to run from. Taurus shows you that only in doing this that you will find a true inner security and a safety in yourself that cannot be touched by anything external – they come from feeling safe and at home inside you.

Use the Scorpio full moon to . . .

✻ **. . . face your shadows.** Be honest with yourself about the parts of you that you try to avoid and hide from. Spend some time with them, understanding the role they have played in helping to keep you safe. Use the waning moon to lovingly release any anything longer need.

✻ **. . . allow things to die away.** What in your life do you need to let go of in order to become more authentic, whole and complete and more at home in yourself? Use the waning moon to gently release anything that you no longer need.

✻ **. . . find an inner safety and security.** Write a list of what makes you feel most safe and secure in life, and ways in which you can provide these things to yourself on a daily basis.

The keywords for Scorpio are 'I DESIRE'

Use this as a journal prompt and see what flows to you in answer. Set some intentions or create some affirmations (see p. 187), using this declaration at the beginning – things like:

✻ I DESIRE deep healing and transformation.
✻ I DESIRE more intimacy in my life.
✻ I DESIRE to live my truth.

What to watch out for under a Scorpio moon:

1 Trying to control or manipulate everything and everyone.

2 Being vindictive and lashing out to hurt; beware of the Scorpio scorpion with the sting in its tail.

3 Making a rash decision to 'destroy'.

 A crystal for this moon: labradorite for revealing truth, danburite for accepting change and leaving the past behind or rose quartz for self-acceptance

CHAPTER 13:

The Moon in Sagittarius

The moon to be a trailblazer

Element: *Fire*
Quality: *Mutable*
Ruling planet: *Jupiter, the King of the Gods*
Symbol: *The Archer*

BRINGING ENTHUSIASM, ADVENTURE, inspiration, passion and a sense of real purpose and freedom, this moon is here to help illuminate your way forward.

MY MOON MUSINGS

A sign of adventure, optimism, faith, awareness and understanding, but notably freedom-seeking, this moon is here to help you to see things clearly – to bring you a new perspective on life. This will be particularly true when it comes to everything that confines and binds you. Any unresolved issues around control, authority, discipline and giving your power away can resurface with this moon.

You may feel literally claustrophobic or suffocated during

this moon when it comes to parts of your life that try to keep you small and stuck or don't allow you your full expression, potential and personal freedom. This moon brings an intense and potent edge as it shines a spotlight on these truths; and if you've been hiding from these things and allowing your voice, passion and potential to be suppressed, you may find this truth difficult to deal with.

If you can lean into what scares you, the discovery of these truths will bring you so much freedom. Straightforward and honest Sagittarius will let you know where your potential is being hidden and your light is being dimmed. This moon will show you in stark reality what is and isn't working in your life and where you are forcing or pretending.

This moon helps you to understand on a deep level why all that has happened has happened, what lessons life has brought you, what part you have played and, especially, how to move on to fulfil your potential. This moon then helps you to lovingly release all that holds you back to make space for new beginnings. Instead of staying stuck and repeating destructive cycles or ways of thinking and being, you can finally free yourself.

And then get ready, as anything can be achieved under a Sagittarius moon. Sagittarius doesn't like the word 'can't' and is here to tell you that you absolutely can – but only if you get clear and honest and see the truth. Focus on what makes you come alive and follow the joy of things that make you feel good. Stop pushing what you cannot control or change – instead, let go and trust in the bigger picture. If you find that you are not where you want to be right now, don't despair. This encouraging, optimistic, personal-freedom-seeking moon is prompting you to be fearless and look towards a bright future.

Sagittarius is motivated by enthusiasm and asks you to be brave and push your ideas, dreams and ideas to the max – and this fiery 'can-do' energy is here to help you to believe it's possible. Sagittarius always keeps one eye on the future and loves a challenge, especially when it comes to setting and meeting goals and targets. So breathe some Sag fire and life back into your dreams. The most loving and peaceful fire sign has come along to light up a flame inside you for positive action, seeking growth, wisdom and happiness.

This is a moon for trailblazers, pushing you towards expansion, meeting your greatest potential and seeing life as an exciting adventure to be fully lived and loved. Sagittarius gives you the confidence to say yes, to accomplish all that you want to and be who you are here to be. Under this moon, you are urged to hear the call of your heart and soul, to find your inner wildness and embrace your adventurous free spirit. Sagittarius wants you to live in freedom, truth and passion and so is fully supporting you in whatever is in your heart right now – whatever brings freedom to your soul and purpose to your life.

THE SAGITTARIUS MOON CALLS YOU INTO . . .

. . . acknowledging where you are and knowing where you want to be; taking aim, drawing back the hunter's bow and releasing the arrows of your intention, dreams and desires; trusting that you have all the means within you to achieve everything you desire – for you are never given a dream without this. This moon brings an influx of possibilities, connections and an ability to see the bigger picture. You are being fully and completely supported towards new beginnings under this moon. Dive into the inspiration, optimism, motivation and liberation that this moon is bringing.

JUPITER, THE KING OF THE GODS, RULES SAGITTARIUS

Expansive Jupiter, the planet of purpose and possibility, wants you to expand your truth, your knowledge and your horizons. This moon will take you to the edge of your comfort zones on a wild adventure to fulfil your greatest potential and seize every opportunity. Jupiter is related to the crown chakra (see p. 30), taking you into the realms of the cosmos and higher consciousness and broadening your vision into what is possible for you this lifetime.

NEW MOON IN SAGITTARIUS FALLS IN SAGITTARIUS SEASON BETWEEN 22 NOVEMBER AND 21 DECEMBER

This begins the last full lunar cycle of the traditional year, and so the Sagittarius new moon is an opportunity for you to review and reflect. What has this year taught you? How have you grown? And in the next year, what are you aiming for?

This moon will bring healing, understanding and truth and is a great opening for change and new beginnings. You may find if you have allowed yourself to be tamed or your freedom or passions to be stifled, that frustration and self-berating may be present under this moon. Don't fall into this trap; rather than looking back with regret, this is a new moon for action, so use its enthusiasm to forge a way ahead.

What would you do if you knew you could not possibly fail? Like the Sagittarius archer, it's time to take aim and draw back your bow. With its feeling of being alive and adventurous, a Sagittarius new moon makes anything and everything feel possible.

Use the Sagittarius new moon to . . .

✻ . . . review the year gone by. Make a list of all the wonderful things you have achieved this year, what you have learned and how you have grown, and also the things you didn't allow yourself to do through fear or other excuses. Then make a second list of anything you can still add some energy to or set in motion through the waxing-moon phase.

✻ . . . begin to get clear on your intention for the next calendar year. Based on the above discoveries of this year, this is a wonderful moon to start to vision and plant the seeds for how you want the next year to be different. Use the waxing moon to start to put some of these foundations in place.

✱ ... **do something brave and bold**. Sagittarius brings confidence and a quest for life experiences, so do something you've been afraid to do all year – maybe finally booking that travelling experience or studying for that new qualification or doing something wild and free!

FULL MOON IN SAGITTARIUS – FALLS IN GEMINI SEASON BETWEEN 21 MAY AND 20 JUNE

This is the last full moon before the summer solstice, when we go into the second half of the traditional year, so it's a huge completion point. This moon is here to illuminate your way forward, helping you to wrap up the first half of the year, tie up loose ends and deciding who you want to be and what you want to create in the second half.

This full moon is about freedom, so a big full-moon light will shine upon all that confines and binds you. Anywhere you feel controlled, whether that's not being able to speak your truth in relationships, being in the wrong job or not doing what you really love, will get highlighted. This full moon then helps you to lovingly release all that holds you back to make space for new beginnings in the second half of the year.

The sun is in Gemini during this full moon, so the themes of Gemini – such as finding truth, making change and incessant questioning – will now be highlighted by this full moon with Sagittarius energy added to them.

If you find your freedom is being stifled under this moon, use the airy Gemini energy to gently question why, how and what makes you feel like this, so you'll know where to begin to make changes. Gemini will help you to find the truth and your voice – and change-loving Gemini mingled with optimistic freedom-loving Sagittarius will help you to clearly see the way ahead.

Use the Sagittarius full moon to . . .

✸ . . . **release all that binds you.** Make a list of all the things in your life that hold you down or keep you stuck. Next, list ways in which, each day over the waning moon, you can loosen these bindings and start to find a little more freedom daily. This could be as simple as finishing work on time once a week, so you get an evening to yourself to do what you want.

✸ . . . **tie up loose ends**. Notice where you tend to stay stuck in the past, repeating the same things or any unfinished business. Use the waning energy of this moon to complete things, so you can find new beginnings.

✸ . . . **declare your intentions for the summer season**. This tends to be a time when we all feel much more free, so use this bold full moon to plan some escapades of your own for the summer season. And use the waning moon to let go of anything that keeps you from adventure.

The keywords for Sagittarius are 'I AIM'

Use this as a journal prompt and see what flows to you in answer. Set some intentions or create some affirmations (see p. 187), using this declaration at the beginning – things like:

✳ I AIM to fulfil my full potential and soul's calling.
✳ I AIM my vision towards my goals and dreams.
✳ I AIM to find freedom in all areas of my life.

What to watch out for under a Sagittarius moon:

1 Becoming easily bored, restless and miserable if you feel restricted in any way.

2 Too much optimism (pretending that everything is ok) to avoid seeing the truth.

3 Wanting to run away from it all and making a desperate, not so well-thought-out dash for freedom.

 A crystal for this moon: chrysocolla for freedom and release, moldavite for fulfilling your potential or amethyst for goal setting

CHAPTER 14:
The Moon in Capricorn

The moon to find structure and focus

 **Element:** *Earth*
Quality: *Cardinal*
Ruling planet: *Saturn, the planet of karma*
Symbol: *The Mountain Goat*

THE AMBITIOUS AND hard-working Capricorn moon likes things to be structured, long-term and future-focused, helping you to find a clear direction to go in.

MY MOON MUSINGS

This moon comes along to shake the foundations of your life – your relationships, career, happiness, goals, dreams, beliefs and the very core of your being. If your foundations are firm, they will stay, but if they are not real and true for you – if it's just not meant to be – they will crumble and fall under this moon.

Use this moon to get very clear on what it is that you want. If you are not sure, write a list of things that you definitely *don't* want in life. This will be extremely clear, as the Capricorn moon can make you a bit of a moaner! Notice your immediate negative responses and what you are moaning about, then flip this around to get to know what you truly do want. You have the power to make absolutely anything happen under this ambitious hard-working moon.

As you feel your life restructuring, please don't struggle, as this will only cause more suffering. Don't cling and grasp. As wise Buddha says: 'You can only lose what you cling to'. If there has been any part of you that wants to play it safe and stay small, this moon will show you why this isn't an option. You can't shrink or hide or pretend under this moon. What you need to let go of in order to move into your greatness and most fulfilled happiness will become too clear to avoid.

The real magic to all this shifting around is that it adds potential and structure to your dreams and ambitions. This moon is helping you to build a lasting life of happiness. You don't want to live a life on unstable foundations, never knowing when it may fall. As one stone falls out, replace it with something new and lasting that creates even more happiness and will weather any storm. This is the time to literally build the life you desire, one belief, one dream, one desire, one act of bravery, one synchronicity, one vision, one affirmation, one step forward at a time.

Sometimes dreams can feel so far away and responsibility, bills, the pressures of society and all the things that hold you back can seem like a mountain too big to climb, that instead keeps you stuck at the bottom. But the truth is that you can have it all. Whoever said you had to choose? You just need to remove any self-imposed limitations, let go of fears and take the first brave step towards achieving a goal or fulfilling a lifelong ambition or dream. The ambitious, motivating Capricorn mountain goat is here to help you scale your own mountain. If you've ever watched a goat climb a mountain, you'll notice how they always find a way, that they don't just plan their next move but are also looking ahead, so nothing prevents them from reaching their goal.

Capricorn doesn't deal well with emotions, so if you feel that you want to shut yourself off and push everyone and everything away around this moon, this is why. You may feel almost numb and empty, yet with a stream of emotion that's deep and still waiting beneath the surface, that you're not sure whether to delve into. This is a huge advantage of this moon. As the raw emotion gets stripped back, it leaves that practical Capricorn energy to deal with all the things that need doing to take you to where you want to go; the life admin, the starting the website or writing the copy or making the flyers or putting together the business plan or looking at the financials – this is what Capricorn moon energy is here to help you do.

Listen to the guidance you receive, trust your intuition and keep checking in with yourself to make sure you are on the right path. Take sure-footed steps, slowly and steadily towards the peak of the mountain, maybe treading a path where others haven't been before, taking a few calculated risks along the way and not allowing obstacles to obstruct you. Life is always supporting you and sending you in the right direction, so if a path seems to be blocked, maybe that's not your way – find another path; there are many ways to get to the top of the mountain.

THE CAPRICORN MOON CALLS YOU INTO . . .

. . . drawing your dreams down into reality and making them happen. This is not a moon for daydreaming; it's for getting very clear on what you want in your life and exactly how you are going to get it. It's a moon of long-term vision that will bring you an increased urge to fulfil aspirations and an ambitious drive like never before. It's about creating lasting change though consistency, commitment and planning. So make that plan. Break your dreams up into clear, manageable steps that you can take every day, week and month to move you forward.

SATURN, THE PLANET OF KARMA, RULES CAPRICORN

Known as the taskmaster of the zodiac, Saturn, the Lord of the rings, wants you to get to work, and work hard! Although once believed to bring complications and difficulties, Saturn is the great teacher of the zodiac, as it pushes you to over-come seeming difficulties to help you to grow. Saturn creates structure and meaning in our lives. Related to the third-eye chakra (see p. 30), Saturn helps you to see how all your actions have a consequence, as well as any karmic connections. Saturn will show you your self-imposed boundaries and limitations, and also bring the discipline, responsibility and productivity that you need to reach your goals.

NEW MOON IN CAPRICORN – FALLS IN CAPRICORN SEASON BETWEEN 22 DECEMBER AND 19 JANUARY

Nature, with her perfect timing, gives us this grounded and earthy new moon around the time of the traditional new year. It acts like fertile soil in which to plant the seeds and set out your intentions clearly for the new year ahead.

The Capricorn new moon brings a sense of ambition and determination and calls you to consider your long-term goals and your heart's desires. Pay attention to what you are being pulled towards and what stirs your soul as this will help create the theme of the year for you. It is also the sign associated with searching for dharma (your life purpose), so focus on what brings you joy and lights you up.

This new moon is here to help you to attune to what your (mountain) path for the year ahead may be, so use its energies to contemplate what you want to experience, share, create and bring to life. Allow your desires, dreams, visions and intentions to begin to create your reality. Get very clear on what you want the next year to bring for you and then, just like the mountain goat, steadily pick out the path ahead, so you can continue to climb and grow throughout the year to reach your full potential.

Use the Capricorn new moon to . . .

✳ **. . . find your dharma**. Ask yourself the burning questions about why you are here and whether you are living your purpose and passion. List all the things that give your life meaning and use the waxing moon to do more of these things daily.

✳ **. . . consider your long-term goals**. List all the things you would like to see happen in a year's time, along with clear timelines of when you will achieve them by. Make a clear action plan for the traditional year ahead.

✳ **. . . turn the 'why' into 'what'**. If you do feel as though everything in your life is shifting and moving around under this moon, don't struggle. Rather than ask, 'Why is this happening to me?' ask, 'What can I learn from this?' and let the guidance of this moon show you the answers. Use the waxing moon to put your learning into motion.

FULL MOON IN CAPRICORN – FALLS IN CANCER SEASON BETWEEN 21 JUNE AND 22 JULY

The first full moon after the summer solstice, the turning point of the year, which asks you to look at where you are in your life, this moon comes along to help you wrap up the old so that you can enter into the new.

Under this full moon you are being asked to look long-term and are being guided towards what is real and lasting for you. Anything that is not meant for your path and will not serve you in your future will start to fall away.

Emotions may be high as you are forced to face what you have been struggling with, learning from, holding on to, hiding behind or from, avoiding or not dealing with. Delve into these feelings and emotions, as they are your signposts towards greater lasting happiness.

The sun is in Cancer during this full moon, so the themes of Cancer – such as feeling safe and protected, nurtured and loved – will now be highlighted by this full moon with Capricorn energy added to them.

If Cancer is the feminine mother energy, Capricorn is the masculine father energy that has come along to propel you forward in your career, your purpose, what you were brought here to do. The sun in Cancer will help you to bring emotions to the surface, using practical Capricorn to make sense of them. This is a wonderful moon for turning your emotions into action.

Use the Capricorn full moon to . . .

✷ . . . get clear on your emotions. Journal on what emotions are coming up for you under this moon. What are they showing you? And what practical steps could you take to move forward with a clear plan?

✴ **... organise your life.** Capricorn loves things to be organised, so you may feel a sudden urge to clear out your wardrobe, tidy your whole house or get your life admin in order. Do it – actively let go of things you don't need through the waning moon.

✴ **... notice your biggest doubts.** Notice them particularly in the context of your ambitions, aspirations and career goals. Capricorn brings huge potential for success but can also be pessimistic and lacking in confidence. Use the waning of the moon to let these limiting beliefs go.

The keywords for Capricorn are 'I USE'

Use this as a journal prompt and see what flows to you in answer. Set some intentions or create some affirmations (see p. 187), using this declaration at the beginning – things like:

✴ I USE my skills daily.
✴ I USE disciplined action to achieve my goals.
✴ I USE long-term visions to make lasting change.

What to watch out for under a Capricorn moon:

1 Putting everything off until it's 'perfect' (this is a real Capricorn sabotage tactic).

2 Overworking to the point of exhaustion.

3 Allowing doubt, fear and lack of confidence to stop you from moving forward.

 A crystal for this moon: smoky quartz for creating strong foundations, blue topaz for understanding and releasing the past or carnelian for ambition and drive

CHAPTER 15:

The Moon in Aquarius

The moon to realign with your purpose

Element: *Air*
Quality: *Fixed*
Ruling planet: *Uranus, the rebellious planet of awakening*
Symbol: *The Water Bearer*

THIS IS A rebellious freedom-seeking moon that helps you to find your greatest vision and purpose.

MY MOON MUSINGS

This moon is about realigning with your purpose and breaking free of chains. But most of all, it's about trust: deep trust in yourself, in life, in the synchronicities and signs that present themselves to you at all times, in the little inner voices that nudge you, in the road less travelled that you keep making excuses not to walk down.

There is a purpose and greatness within you that come from doing what you love to do, whether it's healing, listening, serving, smiling, supporting, caring, creating and/ or offering out your heart and soul to the world. It is said that if a dream or desire or feeling of purpose is put inside you, the means to achieve it are in there too. You just some- times need to dig down to find them – deep beneath the not enough, the too much, society says, they say, etc.

Visionary, humanitarian-focused Aquarius comes along to show you how you can be of service and how your heart's vision and purpose will serve the world. This moon takes you into your full potential and power to heal, create, make change and help in the way that only you can. So find your passion. If you could do one thing every day for the rest of your life, what would that be? What do you do that makes your heart and soul come to life? What makes you feel valued and on purpose? That is your life calling, right there.

The Aquarius moon helps you to see beyond yourself into what the world really needs – and that it needs you. This will often push you to display previously hidden or dormant talents or bring long-buried dreams back to life, as the Aquarius moon wants to know what's the point of having a gift if you don't want to share it? The world needs you in all your authentic, purpose-filled glory. It's time for you to live by the skills and gifts that you have been given, so that you can live on purpose. This is also a moon that's all about connection, collaboration and working together, for we are so much stronger that way, so ask for help if you need it and offer it to anyone else who can use it.

This is an imaginative, idealistic, bigger-picture moon, so you will find your ability to vision and see the future – and you as your greatest self – much easier. Rather than being afraid of and backing away from the future, Aquarius loves to lean into it, so lean with Aquarius into all that's possible and allow your vision to be expanded. This may also mean leaning into some big discomfort and change, as freedom-seeking Aquarius will literally break you free of anything that holds you back or makes you feel stuck or small.

Aquarius is often mistaken for a water sign, but it's actually an air sign, and with its focus on the greatest vision of humanity, you may find that you feel quite emotionally detached under this moon and not willing to include others in your plans. As Aquarius pulls you into a corner to start making those plans, you may crave alone time or a need for space to not have to consider others. Even if this feels uncomfortable, go with it and for a short time allow yourself the space to vision what life could be like if you did live completely on your own terms.

Aquarius is strongly independent and anything that threatens your freedom will be obvious under this moon. You will want to rebel left, right and centre. You'll fight for your rights under this moon, and not only yours but everyone else's around you. You will crave distraction from monotony and everyday life and find yourself more spontaneous than usual. You'll yearn for freedom in all its forms, and that makes this moon a good time to make big changes, let go of old beliefs and habits and find more of what makes you you.

THE AQUARIUS MOON CALLS YOU INTO . . .

. . . fearlessly seeking your truth and, primarily, finding an unwavering faith in where your journey is taking you. This moon is like a universal compass pointing you in the right direction. You need to let go of who you believe yourself to be to allow yourself to become who you are. Let go of expectation, worry and fear and follow Aquarius into a brand-new adventure.

URANUS, THE REBELLIOUS PLANET OF AWAKENING, RULES AQUARIUS

Uranus calls you to seek personal freedom, no matter the cost. Uranus will bring brilliant insights, inspired change and a need to be accepted for exactly who you truly are, along with life-altering transformations where they are needed most. So be prepared for change. Trust in the bigger picture and that this is happening *for* you not *to* you.

NEW MOON IN AQUARIUS – FALLS IN AQUARIUS SEASON BETWEEN 20 JANUARY AND 18 FEBRUARY

This new moon falls around Imbolc, the cross-quarter festival that celebrates the first emergence out of winter towards spring.

This moon may have you feeling like you are suspended in time, everything yet nothing, quiet, immersive and in the dark-moon feelings of wanting to hide away. Just as nature stands on the edge of time before tipping over into the first signs of spring, that's what this new moon will do for you.

If you are living in alignment with your purpose and truth, this will feel like an exciting time as Aquarius brings a dreamy, freedom-seeking quality and with it sparks of inspiration and clarity, new ideas and visions. If you aren't, this could be a tricky time as you are called to remove all the weeds, which are preventing your growth.

Use the Aquarius new moon to . . .

✸ **. . . take some time out alone.** This is not a moon for rushing into things and you may find yourself craving time alone. Allow yourself an emotional reset, to feel your way into your own sense of inner power and strength, to be open to change and a shift in ways of not only doing but also being.

✸ **. . . tune into what's stirring.** This is a moon for listening to and feeling your true soul's calling, deep beneath the shouting wants and needs of the mind and ego. What is stirring within you right now and what wants to begin to grow?

✸ **. . . get into alignment with your purpose.** What is your offering to the world? Make a list of your biggest gifts and talents, your passions and desires and what truly makes you come to life. Begin to do more of these things daily through the waxing moon.

FULL MOON IN AQUARIUS – FALLS IN LEO SEASON
BETWEEN 23 JULY AND 22 AUGUST

This full moon is here to help you to untangle, release, experience revelation and to see the truth. This moon will help you to make a clean break, so that you can step into what your brightest future can be and see how you can serve in the world if you lean in and trust.

There is a tendency under an Aquarius full moon to want to stand up for yourself and say what you mean, especially when it comes to areas in your life where you are kept stifled or feel you have no freedom. Try not to have these conversations under the full moon, as emotionally cool Aquarius could have you saying things you don't necessarily mean. These conversations will land much better if you wait for the waning moon.

The sun is in Leo during this full moon, so the themes of Leo – such as living from the heart and your unique spark – will now be highlighted by this full moon with Aquarius energy added to them.

With the sun in Leo, the ruler of the heart, and the moon in cool, emotionally detached Aquarius, the trick to this moon is to bring what is in your heart up into your head, so it can be lived as well as felt. Leo asks you to step into you and start to shine. Aquarius is all about the greater vision for your contribution to the world at large and everyone around you. Aquarius will help you to take what's in your heart and begin to share it with the world.

Use the Aquarius full moon to . . .

❋ **. . . link your head and your heart.** Write a list of all your heart's deep stirrings and callings, along with an action for each that you can take over the waning moon to get your message out into the world.

❋ **. . . make a clean break.** Make a list of any areas of your life, relationships and situations that you find yourself in that stifle your freedom or hold you back. Have these things run their course? And is it time to let them go over the waning moon?

❋ **. . . prepare for change.** The Aquarius moon will show you clearly how you will want to rebel and create more freedom in your life. Make a list of small changes you can implement, bit by bit, over the waning moon, to bring a bigger overall change.

The keywords for Aquarius are 'I KNOW'

Use this as a journal prompt and see what flows to you in answer. Set some intentions or create some affirmations (see p. 187), using this declaration at the beginning – things like:

❋ I KNOW my service to humanity.
❋ I KNOW what I need to do to find freedom.
❋ I KNOW what change is needed.

What to watch out for under an Aquarius moon:

1 Running for the hills in a bid for freedom.

2 Radical views that you try to push on everyone else around you.

3 Rebellion for rebellion's sake.

 A crystal for this moon: moldavite for following your purpose, apatite for humanitarian pursuits or rutilated quartz for helping you to see the bigger picture

CHAPTER 16:

The Moon in Pisces

The moon to dream and believe

Element: *Water*
Quality: *Mutable*
Ruling planet: *Neptune, the god of the sea and planet of inspiration and dreams*
Symbol: *The Fish*

THIS WATERY MOON will put you right in touch with your intuition and your deepest emotions to help you navigate the way forward.

MY MOON MUSINGS

You'll probably feel the Pisces moon building for days, causing tidal waves of raw, sensitive emotions. This last sign of the zodiac will bring an ending to create a new beginning.

This is a moon of true healing, as the gentle waters of the Pisces moon help to soothe, cleanse and renew your emotions. If you can allow yourself to take a thorough emotional cleanse, find forgiveness and look your fears in the eye, this moon will be like a balm for your heart and soul, as it brings deep insights, awakenings, growth, answers. But especially, it calls back home to yourself all of the parts of you that have been scattered – parts you have given away to those who did not appreciate or deserve them. It's a homecoming. A completion.

Mystical Pisces is the keeper of imagination and dreams, so under this moon your imagination will be your most powerful tool. Use it to help you daydream what is possible and what you most want from life. Pisces also has a wonderful ability to romanticise life, so you'll be able to create a world where all is perfect, in your imagination.

As idyllic as this sounds, it comes with a small word of warning: your dreaming needs to be rooted in something real. Pisces can get so caught up in the spiritual realms of 'leaving everything to the universe' that you can forget that you also need to take action and meet the universe at least halfway. The symbol of Pisces is perfect for this moon – two fish swimming in opposite directions: one in the higher realms and one grounded in reality.

Pisces will give you the ability to drift off into daydream fantasies and visualise all that you want your life to be. It will help you to vision what is possible for you, but you need to blend your higher consciousness – the dreaming and the guidance you receive from your higher self and the universe – with real-life human action. While it's true that the universe is on your side, helping you in every moment, *you* have the ultimate responsibility over your own life and destiny. You have to heed the intuitive niggles and nudges and signs the universe gives you and act on them.

Under this moon, as well as being sensitive to your own emotions and needs, you will feel yourself extremely sensitive to those of everyone around you, feeling everybody's feelings and wanting to help. If you are an empath in daily life anyway, you may find yourself under this moon giving all your time and energy away to other people and leaving nothing for yourself.

Pisces isn't very good at boundaries, but that's what you must do to take care of you under this moon. You may also be more susceptible to other people's opinions. This could lead you to distrust your own inner feelings. And that's what Pisces is empowering you to do – to trust.

Pisces will bring the mystical and the magical, the psychic and intuitive, the ability to manifest and create. Your intuition, imagination and deep inner knowing will be extremely strong under this moon, as Pisces calls you into trusting your inner niggles of what is/isn't working in your life. Deep down, you do know what to do; you really do. You know what you want to create and where you want to go, and you know what you need to let go of. Trust in that.

Pisces also asks you to trust in the flow of life – in the fact that everything is happening 'for' you, to help you to grow and evolve and move in the direction you are meant to go in. Even when it comes to the endings, and even if you can't see why it's unfolding the way it is, or the bigger picture – just trust. Under this moon you will just know.

THE PISCES MOON CALLS YOU INTO . . .

. . . allowing endings to create new beginnings. You can't always control how the tides of life flow, but it is up to you how you react to them and whether you fight or flow with life. If you don't like where you are, stop treading water there. Stop clinging on to old relationships, jobs, fears and ways of looking at and believing in life. If life feels like a struggle, then stop swimming upstream and fighting against it. Drop the burdens of fear, doubt, blame, shame, expectation, resentment and guilt that drag you underwater. Let go, let go and allow the flow of life to lead you to where you need to be. This moon is like coming up to the surface and taking a huge, deep breath of fresh air.

NEPTUNE, THE GOD OF THE SEA AND PLANET OF INSPIRATION AND DREAMS, RULES PISCES

If your life could be any way that you wanted it to be right now, what would that look, feel and sound like? Use Neptune's idealistic imaginative qualities to see your dreams in full colour with surround sound. See it, feel it, believe it – and remember that if you can see it and believe it, you can also achieve it. These dreams only come to you because, on some level, they are already real; you just need to follow your intuition and the signs to bring them into this physical reality.

NEW MOON IN PISCES – FALLS IN PISCES SEASON
BETWEEN 19 FEBRUARY AND 20 MARCH

The last sign of the zodiac, watery, intuitive, wise, gentle Pisces is here to draw your awareness inwards for deep healing, so that you can wrap up the astrological year.

This dark-moon time can often come with an influx of huge emotional swelling, old wounds rising to the surface, lessons you have been ignoring coming back up and a desire to run – run as fast as you can and escape your reality.

Watch carefully for the signs in the next few days. This is a moon of deep intuition, and so if you tune in and watch for/follow the signs, it can literally lead you out of the darkness into the (moon)light. Even if you can't quite see the path ahead yet, listen and trust that the waxing moon is lighting the way and all will become clear.

Use the Pisces new moon to . . .

* **. . . reflect on the year gone by**. Reflect not only on the astrological year that's about to come to an end, but also the traditional one. Have you already lost your way since the year began? What can you do under the waxing moon to get back on track and start to move forward?

* **. . . trust in life**. Spend some time journaling (see p. 191) around some of the more difficult times you've had and what you learned or how you grew out of them. Can you see the lessons and blessings in the difficult times? Can you see how you've grown? Can you allow yourself to believe that everything had a

purpose and plan and that every decision has led you to this moment?

✹ **. . . follow the signs**. Once you have set your new-moon intention in motion watch for the signs and act upon them. This is also a moon that lets you know you are not alone and that there is something greater at work. If you really can see no way forward and the signposts are not at all clear, then ask the moon and universe for help and guidance, to show you the direction.

FULL MOON IN PISCES – FALLS IN VIRGO SEASON
BETWEEN 23 AUGUST AND 22 SEPTEMBER

This moon and the questions it brings could have stirred up some deep emotion and a need to hide away or make some dramatic change. But that, in itself, is a blessing. As the saying goes, 'You can't get to your future while your past is still present'.

Don't suppress. This is the moon under which to acknowledge resentments or hurts that cause you to act in certain ways, to find peace with the past, to let go of blame and a victim mentality and, ultimately, to find acceptance and forgiveness in the present moment.

This Pisces full moon is the last full moon before the season turns and we move into autumn. So use the illumination of this full moon to look back over all that has happened since the summer solstice back in June – the journey you have been on, the lessons learned and what has challenged and changed you.

The sun is in Virgo during this full moon, so the themes of Virgo – such as grounding, practicality and analysis – will now be highlighted by this full moon with Pisces energy added to them.

The sun in real, grounded, practical Virgo, will help you not only to balance out deep emotional impulses with profound understanding, but also your intuitive knowing with real action towards what you want to achieve. This is a powerful combination.

Use the Pisces full moon to . . .

✴ **. . . close off the season.** This full moon is a huge turning point, and this watery final sign of the zodiac will help you to move into the next season, shedding the old, releasing anything that does not serve you and tying up loose ends. What do you need to let go of under the waning moon?

✴ **. . . forgive.** Remember, forgiving does not mean that you are saying that what other people have done to you or where life has brought you is ok, but rather that you are no longer willing to carry around the burden of those hurts and emotions. Make a list of all the people you want to forgive, including yourself.

✴ **. . . allow your emotions to surface.** This helps you to come out on the other side, into the next season, more healed and whole – because as long as you keep suppressing or ignoring your emotions, hiding or staying in denial, you can't heal. And this moon is here to help you to heal.

The keywords for Pisces are 'I BELIEVE'

Use this as a journal prompt and see what flows to you in answer. Set some intentions or create some affirmations (see p. 187), using this declaration at the beginning – things like:

✳ I BELIEVE in my visions and dreams.
✳ I BELIEVE in the voice of my intuition.
✳ I BELIEVE in the guidance and support from the universe.

What to watch out for under a Pisces moon:

1 Becoming emotionally irrational and magnifying your fears completely out of proportion.

2 Getting so caught up in illusion and imagination that you lose touch with the real world.

3 Waiting to be rescued, rather than taking action to manifest things in your own life.

 A crystal for this moon: agate for emotional healing, malachite for endings and beginnings or iolite for dreams and imagination

PART III:

Delve Deeper into Your Moon Practice

CHAPTER 17:

Moon Rituals and Reflections

ONE OF THE greatest gifts that Lunar Living gives us is the opportunity for ritual.

We have so many routines in life, but we have lost rituals along the way. Routine is mundane, expected, externally motivated and tends to be done out of duty or a need to get something done. When we get caught up in routine we very rarely stop to listen. Life simply becomes one to-do list after another and we coast along in a linear way, skimming the surface and living from the outside in. We never delve beneath the surface, listen to the voice of our intuition, the signs and signals, our deepest desires.

Ritual, however, is what makes something meaningful, symbolic and gives life value. It's how we tend to our inner world and hear the whispers of our own souls. When we begin to live by ritual, life takes on a whole new meaning. We start to live from the inside out. Our inner dreams and desires affect, shape and mould our outside world and life acquires a magical quality, a sense of purpose and deeper connection.

New- and full-moon days give us the opportunity for ritual,

for marking a passage of time, keeping ourselves accountable and moving in the right direction. They are marker points within a month where, no matter what else has been happening in your life, you can come back home to yourself, under the guidance of the moon, to reflect, reconnect, realign and refocus if need be.

One of my main passions in life is to keep things simple – to do them in ways that can easily fit into everyday life. So below you'll find simple ideas for working with the energies of the new and full moon, to keep yourself aligned with your lunar rhythm and flow.

You can always deepen these practices by adding the different elements of the sign the moon falls in and, of course, make these into even bigger ceremonies or gatherings (see Chapter 18 for more moon magic and help with using crystals, candles, affirmations and visualisations and other ideas for marking moon days). Remember that you cannot get this wrong and, over time, you will develop your own way to stay connected to the rhythm and flow of the moon and your life.

I have also included some suggested moon reflections under each of the moon phases in Chapter 3 and on the following pages for each new and full moon. Reflect on the questions and allow the wisdom and guidance of the moon to reflect back to you the answers from within. Don't overthink them. Instead, imagine the wise moon in the sky above you, take a moment to feel her energies and open yourself up to receiving her wisdom and guidance. You may take a moment to ask her for any advice or inspiration. Then open your eyes and write the first thing that comes to you.

NEW-MOON RITUALS

The new moon is the time to decide on what you want to create in your life for the following lunar cycle. You can use the new-moon reflection prompts on the next page to help you get clear on this and create some affirmations and a visualisation (see p. 189) to use during the waxing-moon cycle. Once you have these, light your moon candle (see p. 143 for more on this) and repeat aloud your new-moon intentions and affirmations. Then sit quietly with your candle and do your visualisation. Once you have finished, gently blow out your candle, imagining all your new-moon dreams and wishes being released into the world.

As the new moon is the beginning – a blank slate – this is a wonderful time for a cleansing ceremony to ensure that you start afresh, cleansing not just your environment but also your physical, emotional and spiritual bodies. Use a Palo Santo or sage smudge stick around your home to clear and cleanse your surroundings, making sure that you send the smoke into all the corners of your rooms and feeling any old or stuck energy being released. You may even repeat to yourself that you are clearing out the old to welcome in the new. Use frankincense oil to cleanse your aura and energy by placing a few drops in your palms. Rub your hands together before bringing them over the nose and deeply inhaling, then run your hands all around the outside of your body, visualising that you are clearing your emotional and energy bodies of anything that is stagnant or stuck. You can do this daily over the waxing cycle.

New-moon reflections

✻ Since the last full moon what has shifted for me?

✻ What, if anything, have I let go of?

✻ What are the main emotions I have been experiencing in the last few days of the dark moon?

✻ What has this shown me?

✻ What do I want to create in this next lunar cycle?

My intention for this lunar month is:

....

....

Three actions I will take during the waxing moon to move me further towards my intention are:

1. ....

2. ....

3. ....

My affirmations for this waxing moon are:

1. ....

2. ....

3. ....

Any final guidance and wisdom from the moon, or things I feel called to write down?

....

FULL-MOON RITUALS

The full moon is the midway point of the lunar month, when things start to come to completion, and we get to see clearly what has stood in the way. Use the full moon reflections on the next page to get clear on where you are at this stage in the lunar month and what you need to release during the waning moon. Once you have done this, you can create some waning-moon affirmations and light your candle (see p. 193). As you close your eyes and breathe deeply, exhale out of your mouth, visualising that you are letting go of all that needs to be released. When you have finished, gently blow out your candle and imagine that you are fully releasing all that you need to let go of.

As the full moon is the releasing time of the lunar cycle, a burning ceremony can be extremely powerful. Write down all that you want to release – I often find it helps to write each thing on a separate piece of paper –then hold each piece to your heart, one at a time, and state what you want to release, before setting it alight and dropping it into a fireproof dish (safety first!), feeling the fire burn away all that you want to let go of.

Full-moon reflections

✴ What are the main emotions I have been
experiencing in the run-up to this full moon?

✴ Since the last new moon what has shifted for me?

✴ What has moved me towards the goals I set myself
on this new moon?

✴ What has stood in the way or felt difficult? (This is
what you need to process under this full moon, to
shine a light on and release.)

This full moon is shining a light on:

....

....

Three actions I will take during the waning moon to help
me release things that stand in my way are:

1. ....

2. ....

3. ....

My affirmations for this waning moon are:

1. ....

2. ....

3. ....

Any final guidance and wisdom from the moon, or things
I feel called to write down?

....

Moon magic made easy

New- and full-moon days give us the opportunity for ritual and reflection so we keep ourselves accountable.

✴ On each new- and full-moon day reflect on what has happened since the last moon so that you can be sure that you are moving in the right direction.

✴ A new moon is for cleansing rituals and setting intentions.

✴ A full moon is for releasing rituals and letting go.

CHAPTER 18

Furthering Your Practice and Discovering More Moon Magic

Once you have got used to working with the energies of the new and full moons, and perhaps some of the other phases in between, it's time to add a little more magic. Here are just a few ways you can add to your moon rituals, bringing even more potency to your moon work.

CRYSTALS AND THE MOON

Incorporating crystals is an incredibly simple way to enhance your moon practice. Crystals come from the earth (although some also fall from the skies) and each one carries a different healing power, vibration and energy, which you can use to enhance your moon magic.

On the night of the new or full moon, repeat aloud or whisper into your heart your moon intentions while holding your chosen crystal. Ask your crystal for any support, wisdom, guidance or help in any of the areas in which you need it. Then wear your crystal or keep it nearby and try to meditate with or just hold it for a few moments daily. Every time you touch your crystal it will keep amplifying your moon intentions, reminding you of them and helping you bring them to life.

Below are some common crystals, and I have also given you some specific crystal suggestions for the moon in each zodiac sign (see Part II). These are only for guidance though – it's important to use your own intuition when choosing crystals; trust that you will choose the right one for what you need. And remember to put your crystals out under the full moon to cleanse and charge them.

✴ **Moonstone** If you're just starting out on your crystal journey, moonstone is a wonderful one to begin with. As the name suggests, it carries the energy of the moon and will help you to bring your moon intentions to life.

✴ **Clear quartz** This is known as the master crystal, due to its extremely versatile properties and high vibration. It will greatly amplify all your intentions, making it one of the best to use when intention-setting.

✴ **Rose quartz** This is the crystal of love. If you are working on love of any kind, including self-love and belief that you deserve what you want, or any issues of the heart like heartbreak or feeling closed or stuck, this is the crystal to use.

✴ **Citrine** A powerful crystal of manifesting and abundance, citrine is also associated with the solar plexus, your place of personal power, helping bring the confidence, power and self-belief that you need to achieve your goals and dreams.

MOON-TIME AFFIRMATIONS

Affirmations are powerful tools to assist with your moon magic. Repeated over and over again, they help you to overcome doubts, fears and negative self-talk and to truly believe in your wonderful self, your gifts and abilities and what you want to create in your life.

I would suggest that you use three affirmations at a time – any more can be too much – and repeat each one at least three times, morning and evening. The more you repeat them, the more power you will give them. If you can say them looking in a mirror, you will add even more power.

Affirmations need to be in the present tense, contain only positive words (so rather than 'I release doubt', you'd say 'I trust in myself'), be specific and clear and, most of all, mean something to you. I also find it helps to keep them short and sweet, so you get right to the point.

New-moon affirmations

These will be based upon the intention/s that you set yourself on the new moon around what you want to create in your life. Think about what you would need to do, receive or believe to take you closer to your new-moon intentions and dreams and create affirmations based on that. Use the affirmations daily through the waxing part of the cycle to keep adding energy to your intentions and bring them to life. Here are some examples:

✴ My ideal job comes to me easily and effortlessly.
✴ I easily make the connections I need to bring my new business to life.
✴ I am worthy and deserving of love.
✴ I trust my intuition to guide the way.

Full-moon affirmations

These will be based upon what the full moon shone a light on, and what you realised stood in your way and what you need to release. Remember that affirmations need to be in the positive present tense, so take what you want to let go of and find the opposite. Here are some examples:

✴ If you realised during the waxing moon that you tend to procrastinate as a sabotage tactic, your affirmation may be: 'I am productive and get things done right now'.
✴ To let go of fears and doubts, find the opposite and affirm it: If you feel scared say 'I am brave and bold'. If you doubt your abilities, try 'I believe in myself'. If you are struggling to give or receive love say 'I love and approve of myself'. The more you affirm the opposite, the more it will come true for you.

You can also refer to Chapters 5–16 for suggested affirmations beginning with the relevant keywords for each zodiac sign. Use these keywords to amplify the energy of a particular moon, adding your own affirmations to them.

VISUALISING AND MANIFESTING WITH THE MOON

Visualisation is a powerful technique and, used alongside affirmations, it can really help you to achieve your goals. Visualisation is best started on a new moon, as this is the beginning of the lunar cycle and the most powerful time to get clear on what it is that you want out of life.

Once you know what you want to visualise and manifest, write it down on the night of the new moon. It doesn't have to be specific – just bullet points or notes on what your goal or dream looks like. Now, here's the important part: write down how this coming true would make you feel. Go into as much detail about the feeling as you can. Feelings are not only the secret ingredient in your visualisations – but also remember that in Chapter 2 we talked about feelings being your signposts. So once you are clear on how you want to feel, this can become your inner compass: when you are unsure about anything, ask whether it takes you closer to or further away from that feeling.

Once you have this picture in your mind and feeling in your heart, you're ready for the visualisation part:

✴ Sit or lie somewhere comfortable.

✴ Take a few long, slow, deep breaths to relax and centre yourself. Become as present in your body and breath as you can be.

✴ When you feel relaxed, start to imagine that you have whatever it is that you want – as though it's true, right here, right now. Not only that, but with your entire heart feel, as though you already have it, as though this movie you are playing in your mind is absolutely real. Make it full colour, surround sound, HD, adding as much feeling and detail to it as you can. Truly see, feel and experience it.

✴ Ask the moon to guide you towards what you need to do to make this dream a reality, and then follow the guidance you receive.

Repeat this visualisation daily through the lunar month, even if it's just for a few minutes. Use your emotional compass to help you gauge when you are on or off track. Under the bright illumination of the full moon, check in with how you may be holding yourself back or not living and acting in accordance with your vision. Readjust if necessary. Once the dark moon comes around again, take some time to notice how things shifted and took you towards what you wanted, and what changes you now need to make to your visualisation for the next lunar month.

A MOON JOURNAL

A journal specifically dedicated to your moon practices can be very useful. Journaling under each new and full moon, or each of her phases or even daily, is such a powerful tool of self-enquiry and self-awareness. You will begin to discover how different moons affect you and notice feelings, intentions and goals that you find yourself coming back to again and again. You will start to see what you have created and manifested as you set your intentions and work towards goals with the moon's guidance.

Use your moon journal for your reflections (see Chapter 3 and 17); this way, you can look back and see what has shifted and changed for you moon by moon. Write your visualisations and affirmations in here too. You can also use the keyword of each zodiac sign as a journal prompt for the new/full moon. Write it across the top of your page and see what flows out in response.

A MOON ALTAR

A moon altar can be a simple, small space in your home where you go to honour the cycles of the moon, meditate and perform your rituals. It can contain anything that's meaningful for you and reminds you of the cycles of the moon and nature. You may change it every moon or season, with things that represent that time. Writing out your moon intentions and affirmations and keeping them in a sacred place on your altar will add more power to them. You can also keep your crystal on top of them to keep amplifying the energy. If there are things that you are working on and towards with your moon intentions, you can keep pictures and representations of these things on your altar to symbolise what you are bringing into your life.

A MOON BATH (OR SHOWER)

There are two ways this can be done, and both help to bring you into a deeper, more aware connection with moon days.

You can stand outside underneath the moon, especially a full moon (with the new moon, you won't see her in the sky, but her energies are still there and powerful). Feel the energies of the moon in the sky above you and bathe in them. Feel them showering down all around you as you breathe and soak in the power, energy and brightness. Ask for any guidance that you may need and feel her energy soak into every cell of your body, filling you with her wisdom, light, guidance and power.

You can also use a physical bath or shower on a new- or full-moon night. Light some candles, add crystals, flower petals, your favourite aromatherapy oils, salts and scrubs. Turn this into a ritual and a sacred time out from your busy life.

* Under a new moon see this as an act of self-care, preparing you for the month ahead. Use the time as you soak to think clearly about the next lunar month, work through your visualisations and repeat your affirmations.

* Under a full moon, take time to process the first half of the cycle, where you are right now and perhaps where you may have strayed from your new-moon intentions. Ask the waters to cleanse away anything that no longer serves you and to wash away any fears.

MOON CANDLES

 Buy yourself a candle – it doesn't have to be expensive, just a basic pillar candle will do. On the new moon, light your candle and tell it all your new-moon wishes. Sit with your candle for a few minutes, either doing your visualisation or gazing gently into the flame. When you have finished, gently blow it out and imagine that you are sending all your new-moon wishes out into the world. Repeat this daily through the waxing-moon cycle.

You can also light your candle on the full moon (you may wish to use different candles for the new and full moons). Speak into your candle all that you want to release and let go of. Sit with your candle for a few minutes, feeling as though you are letting go with each breath. Once you have finished, gently blow out the candle and imagine that you are breathing out and away all that you want to release. Repeat this daily through the waning-moon cycle.

MOON CIRCLES

There are few things more powerful than gathering together under a new and full moon, with a shared intention. When I see what the women in my Lunar Living online sisterhood create and achieve through our circles, and the beautiful, nourishing support they give each other throughout the cycles, I know this to be true. There is so much magic and collective power in coming together under the moon and sharing intentions, hopes, dreams and even problems and doubts and fears, while receiving the support of other women.

This could simply mean meeting up with your best friend or a group of girlfriends to draw upon the energy and power of the moon together. Imagine having the collective energy of all your girlfriends behind your intentions and everyone helping and supporting each other. There are no rules as to what a moon circle needs to be, but it's important that it feels safe and powerful. Some basics may be an altar in the middle of the circle, allowing each person space to share and offer or receive support, setting intentions, a group meditation to amplify these intentions and a holding space to receive the energy and guidance of the moon. Give it a try and see what works best for you. You might also use some guidance from the new and full moon rituals in Chapter 17.

Moon magic made easy

✴ Crystals will help amplify your intentions and work through the lessons of each moon.

✴ Affirmations are powerful tools to assist you with your moon magic.

✴ Visualisation used alongside your affirmations will really help you to achieve your goals.

✴ A moon journal will help greatly with self-enquiry and self-awareness.

✴ A moon altar will give you a sacred space in which to perform your moon rituals.

✴ A moon bath will help you to connect to and draw down the energies of the moon.

✴ Moon candles will assist you in sending your moon intentions out into the world.

✴ Moon circles are a powerful way of connecting under the energies of the moon.

CHAPTER 19:

Blue Moons, Black Moons, Retrogrades and Eclipses

EVERY NOW AND then you may hear about a supermoon, a blue moon or that we are in eclipse season. And of course, we can't forget about Mercury retrograde. Here is what you need to know to understand these terms and how they affect your moon magic.

BLUE AND BLACK MOONS

Typically, there is one new and one full moon in each calendar month. However, sometimes two moons fall within one month and the extra moon would be known as a black (new) and blue (full) moon. The same terms also apply to an extra moon in a season. Each season (spring, summer, autumn and winter) usually has three new and three full moons, but occasionally there will be a fourth. When this happens the third moon in the season is a black or blue moon. These two occurrences happen every two to three years.

A rarer occurrence is when February has no new or full moon, and so January and March will tend to have two. This happens every 19 to 20 years.

You've probably heard the saying 'once in a blue-moon' – well, that's what this moon brings: a once-in-a-blue moon opportunity for change and transformation. A blue moon adds extra energy to the already potent illuminating power of a full moon, helping you to clearly see all the things that you put off doing and how you can take steps towards making them happen. This could be anything from changing jobs, taking a leap of faith into starting a new venture, leaving an outdated relationship or finally taking that trip you've been talking about. The blue moon helps you to see why you have been putting these things off and gives you that once-in-a-blue-moon chance to change things.

New-moon energy is greatly amplified on a black moon; it's a time for a new beginning. It usually helps to look at what the first new moon of the month brought for you, as this will lay the groundwork and set the tone for the following black moon. A black moon will often bring a big release, creating space for what you want to manifest. Your new-moon intentions will be amplified and backed by extra power and potential, so make sure that you dream big on a black moon.

SOLAR AND LUNAR ECLIPSES

A solar eclipse can only happen on a new moon, as the moon passes between the earth and the sun, blocking out the sun.

A lunar eclipse can only happen on a full moon, as the moon passes directly behind the earth, blocking the light of the sun from shining on the moon.

A blood moon happens during a lunar eclipse when refracted lights from the earth's atmosphere make the moon appear red.

Eclipses usually tend to happen twice a year and come in seasons, which last about 35 days. During this eclipse season there will be two or three eclipses, so any full or new moon occurring in this season will be an eclipse. The time between these eclipses is known as a gateway and is a magical, powerful time of growth and change.

Eclipses tend to come along to reveal truths, bring things to your attention and help put you back on the right path, creating endings and new beginnings. The energy of eclipses can often be quite deep and intense, but they are powerful portals for huge transformation and opportunities for growth.

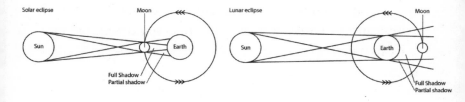

SUPERMOON

The moon doesn't orbit around the earth in a perfect circle, but more of an elliptical or oval shape, so at certain times of the month she is closer to the earth than at others. When the moon becomes new or full in a point closest to the earth it is known as a supermoon. When a moon is a supermoon her energies are amplified and the effects felt much more strongly, making your moon magic more potent.

MERCURY RETROGRADE

 I can't leave out Mercury retrograde, as it seems to go hand in hand with Lunar Living and can significantly affect all of us, whether we realise it or not.

Three or four times a year for around three weeks at a time Mercury, the planet of communication and technology, appears to move backwards. Known as Mercury retrograde, this phenomenon has had a bad rap over the last few years, since becoming more widely talked about, particularly on social media.

Although this can indeed be a time when things go wrong – technology begins to malfunction, contract signing should be avoided (or at least quadruple-checked), travel plans seem to go awry, you feel indecisive and forgetful and no matter what you say, things seem to be misheard or misunderstood – Mercury retrograde can also be a time of real transformation.

Retrogrades are a time for introspection and reflection, as they take you right into your subconscious, making it a great opportunity to slow down, stop rushing and doing, and tune into your inner world and your intuition – into the feelings and knowings there aren't always words or explanations for in our modern-day world. Those things you just know, without knowing how you know them.

Mercury retrograde can also be a wonderful chance to look at your communication skills in general. Do you truly listen or are you already forming a response to what someone is saying before they've finished speaking? Do you think before you speak? Do you say what you 'think' or how you 'feel'? This can be a great opportunity to take your time, listen, speak from your heart with intent and to really notice where your words come from. Take time over a retrograde to consider what's behind the thousands of words we speak a day – the communication that doesn't need words.

The zodiac sign that Mercury retrogrades in can give you deeper insight into what that retrograde cycle will bring up for you, but generally you may find any unhealed chapters of your life coming back around to be finished off, ex-partners reappearing or that all of your hidden/old fears, shadows and insecurities come to the surface.

The only way through Mercury retrograde is to go with its flow. Don't try to fight against it – that will only make the process harder. And that's what this is, a necessary process. Just as the moon has to go into her dark phase every month to shine her full brightness, sometimes you need to visit the shadows, to slow down, process, catch up and explore your subconscious hidden realms. If you allow this inner process, you'll come out the other side more healed, more whole, more self-aware and more ready to follow your heart and soul.

Moon magic made easy

* A black (new) or blue (full) moon is the second full moon in a calendar month or third in a season that has four moons.
* A blue moon brings an opportunity for change and transformation.
* A black moon brings a big release, creating space for something new.
* A solar eclipse can only happen or a new moon and a lunar eclipse on a full moon.
* Eclipses are powerful portals for transformation and change.
* A supermoon is when the moon is closest to the earth and heightens the energy of the moon.
* Mercury retrograde happens three or four times a year and brings a wonderful opportunity for introspection, reflection and slowing down.

Resources

• • •

To find out more about the current moon phase:
astrocal.co.uk
moonphases.co.uk
kirstygallagher.com

To learn more about astrology:
You Were Born For This by Chani Nicholas (Yellow Kite)

Acknowledgements

• • •

To my wonderful family: Sandra, Kylie, Kerry, Liam, Stephanie, Soraya, Jake, Chloe, Edward, bump and my late Grandpa Donald. I love you and thank you for always loving and supporting me.

To Sam for being the best friend a girl could ever ask for, and to my godson Harley for loving crystals as much as I do. And a big Cwtch to my Welsh family, Selwyn, Janet, Vicki, Chris and Alfie.

My editor, Holly Whitaker, thank you for believing in *Lunar Living* and me, and helping to share my message with the world. And to all the wonderful people at Yellow Kite who have supported me through this journey, thank you. I am so grateful to Myrto Kalavrezou and Caitriona Horne for your PR and marketing skills, Anne Newman for your editing magic and Jo Myler and Casey McCormick for creating the book cover of dreams.

If you are holding this book in your hands, thank you for allowing me to share my passion for *Lunar Living* with you. I hope it changes your life as much as it has mine. I always love to hear from you so please do share your moon magic with me.

My Lunar Living sisterhood, thank you for all your support, lunar love and for being the best sisterhood ever. To Helen Elias, *Lunar Living* would not be what it is without you.

Mel Carlie, thank you for getting me up on stage at the Mind Body Spirit festival all those years ago and for your support ever since. And to the Mind Body Spirit Festival, thank you for always inviting me back.

To the other three of 'The Four', Becki Rabin, Megan Rose Lane and Wendy O'Beirne, thank you for coming into my life and filling it with so much support, love and joy. I thank the multiverse for you all everyday!

Special mentions go to Hannah Holt, Emmaline Turley, Emma Taylor, Laura Williams, Rebecca Dennis, Adele Hartshorn and Ian Steed who supported me during the writing process when I was a recluse!

Gratitude too to Steve Marks for encouraging me in the early days and throughout, John Farrell for always taking care of my website and my lovely friend Ash Radford for your soulful music and playing alongside me in workshops. Also, for the song 'Guided by Waves' which I quoted in Chapter 3 which played on repeat while I was writing this book. Trust in the moon, she whispers we'll be there soon.

To everyone who has allowed me to offer you guidance on your life journey through my soul guidance readings and coaching/mentoring, thank you for your willingness to trust me with your heart and soul. I love seeing you show up in the world.

To all my students and anyone who has ever attended a class, course, retreat or workshop with me, thank you for trusting me with your body, mind, heart and soul. I appreciate you more than you know. And thank you to all my current private clients and corporates for bearing with me through this writing journey, your support and kindness has been invaluable.

To my spiritual home Ibiza, especially the Hotel Catalonia Royal Ses Savines who took such precious care of me during my writing retreat, and Lisa Strong and Anna McColl.

To Harbottle and Lewis, iZettle, Selfridges, Fitbit, Women's Health Live and my lululemon family, thank you for your support. Thank you to Jen Armstrong for all your class cover help while I was writing, and for your wonderful photography skills.

If I have not named you it's not because you are forgotten or that I am not grateful. It's simply that I have been blessed to have so many wonderful people touch my life and not enough pages left to mention you all, it would be another book in itself! If you have ever been a part of my life in any way, thank you.

Finally, my biggest thanks to the Moon, as without her wisdom, support, guidance and ebb and flow, none of this would be possible.

About the author

• • •

Kirsty Gallagher is a moon mentor, soul alignment and transformation coach, yoga teacher and meditation teacher with an infectious passion for life.

She has been sharing the life-changing benefits of yoga and the moon for 10 years through classes, workshops, private and corporate sessions, and has taught over 80 worldwide retreats. She is the founder of the online sisterhood *Lunar Living*, which teaches you how to weave the secret and ancient wisdom of the moon into modern, everyday life.

Kirsty works alongside women helping them live back in alignment with an ancient cycle, a natural rhythm and flow, and she helps them to connect back into their authenticity and purpose. Weaving lunar wisdom with soul guidance readings, astrology and cutting-edge transformational coaching techniques, Kirsty helps women to overcome doubts, fears and self-sabotage to find a deep inner connection and meaning in life.

Alongside a full teaching and coaching schedule, Kirsty consults for and runs a number of corporate wellness programmes, talks and workshops bringing lunar inspired yoga, self-care, stress management, meditation and mindfulness to the business world in an easy to understand way. She is a lululemon legacy ambassador and runs regular workshops (crystal healing, moon magic, stress and resilience, desk yoga, etc.) for Selfridges. She has recently taught yoga on House of Fit for Fitbit and has talked at Mind Body Spirit, Women's Health Live, Om Yoga Show, Wilderness Festival, Sweat and Sound and at lululemon's Sweatlife festival. She is regular contributor for the yoga and wellness press, with her retreats featured in *The Times, National Geographic* and *The Metro,* and her moon magic has been featured in *Women's Health, Top Sante* and *Spirit and Destiny.*

Described as down to earth, warm-hearted, compassionate and inspiring, Kirsty is known for bringing ancient mystical practices and wisdom to modern day life in a relatable way that anyone and everyone can take something from. Find about more at kirstygallagher.com.

Photograph by Jen Armstrong

books to help you live a good life

Join the conversation and tell
us how you live a #goodlife

🐦 @yellowkitebooks
📘 YellowKiteBooks
📌 Yellow Kite Books
📷 YellowKiteBooks